A MASTER GUIDE TO MEDITATION AND SPIRITUAL GROWTH

Roy Eugene Davis is a direct, personal disciple of Paramahansa Yogananda and a widely traveled teacher of meditation and spiritual growth methods.

He is the director of Center for Spiritual Awareness, with headquarters and retreat facility in northeast Georgia and meditation centers in several North American communities and other countries. Mr. Davis is the author of many books and the publisher of *Truth Journal* magazine, which has an international distribution.

A
MASTER
GUIDE TO
MEDITATION
& SPIRITUAL GROWTH

Roy Eugene Davis

CSA PRESS, *Publishers*
CENTER FOR SPIRITUAL AWARENESS
Lakemont, Georgia 30552

CSA Press, Publishers
P.O. Box 7
Lakemont, Georgia 30552

CSA Press is the publishing department of
Center for Spiritual Awareness. Offices and
retreat center located on Lake Rabun Road,
Lakemont, Georgia 30552 (U.S.A.)
Telephone (706) 782-4723

In West Africa:
Centre for Spiritual Awareness
Post Office Box 507, Accra, Ghana

Peter Oye Agencies
Post Office Box 5803, Lagos, Nigeria

PRINTED IN THE UNITED STATES OF AMERICA

I salute the supreme teacher,
the Truth
who is the giver of the highest
happiness,
who is beyond all qualities
and infinite like the sky,
who is beyond words,
who is one and eternal,
pure and still,
who is beyond all change
and phenomena,
and who is the silent witness
to all our thoughts and emotions:
I salute Truth,
the supreme teacher.

— Ancient Vedic Hymn

INTRODUCTION

Awakening to the Heart of Reality

This book was written to serve the reader who is sincerely interested in spiritual growth and willing to be completely committed to intentional practices and transformative processes which they can facilitate.

There are no secrets or mysteries about spiritual growth. It is the natural process of soul—or Self—illumination when conditions are suitable for it to occur. At our core, behind the finest layers of thoughts and emotions, we are forever established in God. Before the beginning of time, we existed as individualized units of pure consciousness, reflections of God's spirit. When the universe no longer prevails, we will continue to abide in God.

Why, then, of the millions of seekers of knowledge, do so few awaken to it? It is because many who seek do not look in the right direction. Or, if they do, their resolve does not take their awareness deep enough—into the heart of Reality. That knowledge and realization of absolute Consciousness-Existence is possible, is verified by the several illumined souls who have appeared on the world scene through the centuries and who have affirmed it by their words and exemplary lives. We need not doubt our spiritual qualifications to demonstrate awakened spiri-

tual consciousness. In truth, as spiritual beings, we are
the same as all souls which have emerged from the Light
of Lights to sojourn for a while in the arena of relative
life.

An earnest inquirer into the truth—and meaning—of
life should be ever mindful of the fact that mind-body identity is temporary—a few score years on Planet Earth and
we return to inner realms from whence we came. Our incarnation into a fleshly body resulted in a blending of our
spiritual nature with matter. The fundamental problem
we have when unconscious of our real Selfhood is that of
having forgotten our origins and, therefore, our divinity.
If we are not yet conscious of our essential, spiritual condition and our relationship with the Infinite, our need is
to learn how to be awake.

The information presented here is for everyone regardless of cultural modes or religious identity or preference.
This is because the focus is upon the inner way, which is
the same for all souls desirous of having awareness restored to realization of wholeness. I emphasize "restored"
because we are already whole: it is awareness that becomes fragmented when identified with delusions (erroneous beliefs) and illusions (misperceptions). It is not that
we have to *become* whole; only that right endeavor, right
spiritual practice, and God's grace, enables us to consciously know and demonstrate our wholeness. Whether
one affirms Christianity, Hinduism, Buddhism, or another
traditional faith, or none, the *way* to Self-discovery is the
same. All beliefs and rituals, which may have value for
one while yet seeking, are transcended with the dawning
of cosmic consciousness and direct knowledge and real-

ization of changeless Reality.

It is of value for a devotee of God to have an intellectual grasp of the totality of consciousness: from the field of unmodified, pure existence, to levels of cosmic manifestation, including the realm of sense-perceived matter. Even a fleeting insight into the processes of world-becoming and evolutionary trends can somewhat free the spirit from the conditioned habit of egocentricity which restricts it. We cannot realistically hope for expanded states of consciousness while, at the same time, harboring a limiting self-view and clinging to attitudes, moods, behaviors, and relationships which confine us.

Mind-enriching metaphysical studies, spiritual practices, and intentional, purposeful actions are necessary to establish order in our lives and provide us opportunity for authentic or genuine spiritual growth. Therefore, all of these themes are included here, with emphasis upon meditation practice. The acquirement of valid knowledge is useful. Rational thinking is helpful. Purposeful living can result in reasonable personal success and give some meaning to our lives. But to plumb the depths of consciousness, contemplative meditation is extolled by enlightened people as the direct way.

Proceed with diligence. Become familiar with the philosophical principles. Practice the recommended meditation procedures to become proficient. Test everything you learn. Prove your knowledge by living up to your highest understanding and demonstrating your abilities. In these ways, patiently and progressively become a knower of truth—the facts of life—and experience the real freedom that higher knowledge allows.

Readers presently interested in mild improvements in their lives—in reducing stress and functioning more effectively—will be pleasantly assisted to these ends as they apply themselves to meditation practice and make necessary adjustments in mental attitude and lifestyle. If aspiration is more soul-directed, there are no limits to the inner transformations which can result or to the unfoldments of knowledge and realizations of transcendental realities which can be actualized.

Knowing how to proceed on the awakening path is the first stage in the process. Following through with determined resolve is the second, which is empowered by choice and assures success. God, being omnipresent, is where we are, as a field of infinite consciousness. God, as the Reality of us, is to be thus acknowledged and apprehended. And there is grace: the influential support of the worlds, which impels us to our highest good and reveals to us itself.

Roy Eugene Davis
Lakemont, Georgia, U.S.A.
March 7, 1994

CONTENTS

Part Four
*How to Know, Realize,
and Express God*

Part One

The Primary Purpose
of Meditation and the
Beneficial Results of
Dedicated Practice

The laws of life can teach us how to live in harmony with the world and with ourselves. When we know what the laws are and conduct ourselves accordingly, we live in lasting happiness, good health, and perfect harmony with all life.

Paramahansa Yogananda

In one sentence I will impart to you the essence of all scriptures: God alone is Real, all else is insubstantial and transitory. The Self (the soul or real nature) is God, and nothing else.

Shankara (8th century)

You can only apprehend the Infinite by a faculty superior to reason, by entering into a state in which you are your finite self no longer—in which the divine essence is communicated to you. It is the liberation of your mind from its finite consciousness. Like only can apprehend like; when you thus cease to be finite, you become one with the Infinite. In the reduction of your soul nature to its simplest self, its divine essence, you realize this union—this true identity.

Plotinus (3rd century)

1

Understanding the Spiritual Growth Process

THE FINAL SOLUTION to all human problems—and the only source of real fulfillment—is within us. Try as we may to satisfy our need for personal freedom and soul contentment by external means alone, success will be ever elusive.

At our innermost level of Being, the real Self of us exists in wholesome purity. Here, untouched by mundane conditions and transitory events, abides undisturbed peace, pure bliss, flawless knowledge, and limitless awareness of absolute freedom. This permanent reality of us can be consciously experienced by the simple, simultaneous acts of acknowledgement and acceptance. When we do this, we are Self-realized: established in clear awareness of our real nature as spiritual beings grounded in an unbounded field of pure Consciousness-Existence which is not other than us. Choosing to turn attention to our essence enables us to effectively experience contemplative meditation and awaken to transcendental realities.

For meditation to be effectively experienced it should be understood for what it is and practiced with that

understanding. The procedure is easy to learn and enjoyable to practice. Easy because natural, and enjoyable
because it provides the satisfaction of measureless peace
along with progressive unfoldments of innate spiritual
qualities and capacities. It allows direct access to subtle
and fine levels of awareness and to fields of knowledge
corresponding to them. Participation in the meditation
process yields beneficial results in proportion to the
attention we give to it. The determining factor of results
is right, regular practice with alert, attentive responsive-
ness to unfoldments that occur. Marginal benefits will be
experienced because of physical relaxation and mental
quieting, so that even beginning meditators will notice
general improvements in mental attitude and overall well-
being. A more useful approach is that of giving full attention to spiritual growth processes so that highest benefits
can be demonstrated or actualized.

Extravagant claims to the contrary, meditation is not
to be thought of as an instant remedy for the everyday
challenges which often attend ordinary self-conscious life,
nor will a few weeks or months of practice result in fully
unfolded spiritual illumination. The satisfying benefits
and improved circumstances that blossom almost from
the outset of establishing a daily meditation routine can
be personally rewarding, as well as reassuring evidence
of the usefulness of practice. Acquiring knowledge of how
to live successfully with enlightened (knowledgeable) purpose, however, is usually only accomplished within the
boundaries of time. Psychological transformation, and
coming to terms with awakened states of consciousness
which often require that we learn new ways of relating to

the world, must also be experienced within the field of time if authentic spiritual growth is to be demonstrated in fact. If this were not so, Planet Earth would already be populated with millions of enlightened, healthy-minded, freely functional human beings—which has not yet occurred. A few thousand more years of evolutionary progress are needed before a true Era of Enlightenment is established.

Meditation, as here presented, is not to be practiced to evoke emotionally satisfying moods, escape into interludes of daydreaming, induce alternate but still illusional mental states, or to endeavor to acquire exceptional powers for self-serving or misguided purposes. When practiced correctly on a regular schedule, meditation removes awareness from limiting conditions of every kind and returns it to ourselves—to the innate state of pure Being. Any life-enhancing unfoldments resulting from practice are but side-benefits manifested because of physical and psychological changes and the influences of awakened spiritual consciousness. These are to be graciously welcomed and accepted but are not to be grasped at, or to be considered of primary value.

Getting Started (or beginning anew)
on the Authentic Spiritual Path

It is helpful to the spiritual growth process for one to remain aware of the essential fact that, as spiritual beings expressing through mind and body, the Self we are is ever outside the constraints of time and circumstances even while we continue to relate to them when identified with the material realms. Our innate wholeness and purity becomes Self-revealed to the extent that we are responsive to soul inclinations to unfoldment and as physical and mental restricting influences are removed, transformed, or transcended.

The removal, transformation, or transcendence, of physical, mental, and emotional obstacles to the natural inclination of soul awareness to flow freely may be accomplished in several ways. Honest self-analysis and determined choice can be helpful. Spontaneous transformations because of constructive endeavors to live with higher purpose can occur. The direct actions of superconscious forces which are influential during meditation and may be instrumental at other times, can effect constructive changes. Unexpected, actions of grace are often experienced. Incidents of redemptive grace are the unfoldments of supportive events and circumstances that occur because of the expressive, nurturing impulses of Spirit which are ever inclined to contribute to our well-being and spiritual growth. The actions of grace are not arbitrary: they manifest whenever there are outlets for expression.

Daily practice of meditation is recommended for anyone who is reasonably healthy-minded and desirous of unfolding latent creativity and spirituality. Such a person is willing to allow useful changes to occur when necessary; and regular, right practice of meditation facilitates useful changes. As higher (clearer) states of consciousness are realized and actualized and psychological transformations occur, new ways of knowing ourselves, and of perceiving and relating to the world, are experienced. One who is resistant to the idea of useful changes may be distrustful of meditation. When this attitude prevails, one may consciously or unconsciously avoid compliance with recommended guidelines for practice of meditation and lifestyle adjustments in order to protect or preserve existing philosophical beliefs, personality traits, habitual modes of behavior, or established relationships which are deemed of value because of sympathetic attachment to them. A spirit of adventure, reinforced by courage to confront the unknown, is extremely helpful to us if we are to meditate effectively, grow spiritually, and live successfully.

If you are a new meditator, the best approach to learning the process is to thoroughly read this book, then choose a practice routine that seems best suited to your psychological temperament, personal needs, and aspirations for benefits and spiritual growth. If you are already a practicing meditator, read this book to review your practice and perhaps learn how to improve it. Once the process is comprehended, only experience provided by intentional practice will suffice to reveal intimate knowledge of meditation and allow natural unfoldments to happen.

In addition to regular meditation practice, it is helpful to adopt lifestyle behaviors which will be supportive of your highest ideals for personal fulfillment and spiritual enlightenment. By doing this, your every thought, mood, action, and relationship will nurture radiant wellness and functional expression in every aspect of your life. Habit-bound, conditioned, self-conscious existence is in opposition to the soul's innate urge to have awareness restored to unrestricted freedom. Therefore, do all you can to assist yourself to be more conscious, more creatively

functional, and in harmony with nature's evolutionary
trends by choosing to live as constructively as possible.

You do not have to be spiritually enlightened to choose
a healthy lifestyle. All that is needed to do this is knowledge of how to proceed (which can be acquired), personal
decision, commitment, and commonsense participation.
To live an unhealthy, disorganized life while hoping for
spiritual practices to work miracles is self-defeating. To
live well, without cultivating awakened spiritual consciousness, is to have a materialistic orientation and be
unfulfilled. The ideal approach is to implement a balanced
routine of activities, provide for supportive relationships
and circumstances, and remain attentive to practices
which nurture spiritual growth.

The master-key to realizing satisfying spiritual growth
is to always live up to the highest understanding that
you have: to put into practice what you know so that you
can experience the truth of it. If knowledge and abilities
are not demonstrated, how can further knowledge and
creativity unfold? A common cause of lack of spiritual
growth is that what is already known is not applied.

When doing anything, you have to ask yourself why
you are doing it. You have to ask: What is life's purpose?
When you do this, you have an opportunity to come to
terms with yourself, your world, and your soul destiny.
You will be better able to make right choices, implement
effective actions, and avoid impulsive or inappropriate
actions when restraint is the better choice. You will discover how to live in accord with life's primary purpose,
which is to unfold and express its full potential. As a willing participant in life's intentional processes you will more

rapidly, successfully experience satisfying spiritual growth.

Your course of action, your spiritual path, is authentic when it facilitates your spiritual growth: soul unfoldment which provides Self-knowledge and realization of God which enables you to freely demonstrate your higher understanding. The path is not the destination—it is only the way. Adhere to it and let it support and assist you until you are fully, spiritually awake, then live a life of service. Some truth seekers begin the quest with good intentions, then become so enamored with the path that they forget its purpose. They settle for a small portion of mental peace and enjoyment of metaphysical studies (and, perhaps, the social satisfaction of keeping company with like-minded friends) and neglect to persist in their aspiration for realization of God. They may become skillful in their practices but forget the reason for their involvement. This will not happen to you if you clearly understand the process of spiritual growth and give yourself to it.

2

The Primary Purpose of Meditation Practice is Self-Realization

SELF-REALIZATION IS CONSCIOUS AWARENESS of ourselves as spiritual beings, validated by our ability to demonstrate awakened soul consciousness and live healthy, creatively functional lives.

Unenlightened people, because of lack of personal knowledge, almost always declare Self-realization to be difficult to experience and express. If we aspire to spiritual growth, and are wise, we will avoid being influenced by false opinions and misguided teachings. We will, instead, respond to our innate urge to soul unfoldment and follow its leading. In fact, what could be more natural for us than to awaken to our real, permanent, spiritual condition? What more honest act could we perform than to directly acknowledge, that what we have long desired to become, we already are? Knowing this, I emphasize the simplicity of Self-realization.

The restoration of soul awareness to its original, fully conscious state should be foremost in the awareness of a dedicated truth student. The demonstrations, the results of Self-realization, are of secondary interest but do provide outer evidence of inner grace. More immediate indications of awakened spiritual consciousness are the spontaneous manifestations of radiant calmness, mental clarity, spontaneity, simplicity, and natural ease in relating to circumstances. A Self-realized person is completely conscious and the effects of their personal presence upon others are morally and spiritually elevating. Even when we think of a Self-realized person, if our intuition is somewhat awakened, our soul forces are enlivened and transcendental perceptions may suddenly unfold. We benefit by acknowledging the expressed, divine qualities of enlightened souls because such recognition reminds of us of, and more obviously awakens, our own.

Why is realization of our true nature so commonly believed to be difficult to experience and express while also acknowledged to be of utmost value to us? The answer is evident in the human condition. Even though at the soul level we are inclined to transcendental awakenings, our inability to easily adjust our viewpoint from illusional concepts and emotional states to clear awareness of our real nature prevents us from having conscious experience of ourselves as free beings. It is normal for persons who are not yet fully awake to the truth to think of Self-realization as being beyond their power to apprehend and actualize.

Yet, the living testimony of enlightened men and women is that it is easy to experience Self-realization when right understanding and right endeavor are coordinated. Whom shall we believe? Shall we accept as true the claims of persons who admit to their incomplete knowledge, or shall we hearken to the words of those whose teachings ring true in our hearts and whose actions demonstrate higher understanding? The choice should not be difficult to make.

Right Understanding Supports
Orderly Spiritual Growth

Many spiritual aspirants, even though sincere, are hopelessly confused because deficient in knowledge about themselves and of what they want to accomplish. They are attempting to actualize their hopes for self-improvement and spiritual growth without knowing how to proceed, often applying the same self-defeating actions which are already contributing to their disorganized, unfulfilled circumstances.

The most obvious way to be assured of success in any worthwhile venture is to seek out sources of valid knowledge. When knowledge is acquired and actions which can result in useful outcomes are applied, satisfactory results can follow. So it is on the spiritual path. When we know what the goal is, and how to become accomplished, we have only to enter into the process.

The absolute truth about us is that we are rays of God's consciousness. As such, we are not ever going to *become* one with God—because, at the soul level, we *are already* established in oneness. If we do not know this, we have to learn to change the way we perceive and know ourselves. The process is that of removing attention (and attachments) from environmental conditions and from physical and mental states while acknowledging our real nature.

Preliminary endeavors to do this may include adjustments in attitude and feeling. The final action is that of implementing a shift of viewpoint which allows apprehension and direct experience of the true Self of us as conscious, pure Being.

The fundamental cause of clouded soul awareness which obscures true knowledge of Self and God is unconscious identification with mental states, moods, sensory perceptions, and objective circumstances. Thus related to outer conditions, we remain attached to them while being only dimly aware of our essential nature and of subjective realities.

Only momentary self-observation is sufficient to inform us that when we are not soul-centered our awareness is usually involved with random thoughts, shifting moods, sensory urges, and varied perceptions. Even when we want to withdraw attention from these circumstances we are not always able to easily do so. For the average person, clouded, conditioned awareness is considered as normal.

When we are in ordinary, self-conscious or egocentric states of awareness, we may falsely assume that perception of events or objects external to ourselves is proof of our being truly conscious. The illusion, the misperception, is: "I think, feel, perceive, and experience, therefore, I am conscious." To believe that our mental or physical perceptions constitute apprehension of the entirety of what is real, is the result of intellectual error. That it is possible to experience awareness without an object—to be aware without the necessity of having external circumstances support awareness—can be easily demonstrated. We have only to withdraw attention from all objects, including emotional states and thoughts, until conscious awareness of existence alone is experienced. To be thus aware is to be conscious of being conscious.

A fleeting episode of being "conscious of being conscious" is not yet Self-realization. It is not yet a state from which we are completely, spiritually knowledgeable and able to demonstrate it by our actions, but it can be a useful initial stage in the spiritual growth process. It can allow us to choose to withdraw attention from circumstances that may be troublesome, moods, and restless thought processes, so that a degree of inner calm is established and a more objective view of conditions prevails. By knowing that we are not our circumstances, bodies, or minds, we are provided an opportunity to determine to live superior to them instead of being overly influenced by them.

Preliminary meditation processes work directly with this fundamental problem of outer identification that blinds us to the truth of ourselves and to perceptions of higher realities. From the beginning of practice, the meditator learns to sit still and internalize attention, causing awareness to withdraw from sense organs and mental transformations and turn back on itself. It is only when internalized attention flows without disturbance to the chosen focus of concentration or transcendental possibilities that meditation actually occurs. Before this, our endeavors to meditate are preparatory and preliminary.

When sufficiently, consciously internalized, the meditator experiences spontaneous unfoldments of relatively pure levels of awareness, referred to as superconsciousness—this, in contrast to the states of consciousness ordinarily experienced: unconsciousness, subconscious states, and normal waking self-consciousness. Superconscious states are degrees of soul awareness, which may be influenced by mental and emotional conditions during preliminary stages of meditation practice.

As meditation progresses, superconscious states become refined. With physical relaxation and internalization of attention, one experiences emotional peace and mental calmness: not as a result of suppression of feelings and thoughts, but as a result of their being quieted. The meditator, while enjoying an interlude of calm, may wonder if it is a valid superconscious episode. After successive practice sessions, confidence improves and beneficial effects of superconscious experiences are noticed and validated. These indicate their usefulness. With acquired proficiency, the meditator learns to abandon self-consciousness to superconsciousness without doubting its authenticity.

With further internalization of attention, awareness of physical sensations and mental transformations ceases. Expanded states of superconscious awareness then naturally unfold. During this phase of meditation practice one can continue to be surrendered to the process, letting the soul's innate intelligence direct it—or contemplation of higher realities can be gently implemented while remaining open and responsive to spontaneous adjustments of states of consciousness in the direction of transcendental realizations. During the process, the meditator is fully alert, is not subject to illusions or hallucinations, and can conclude the practice session at will by deciding to do so.

When superconsciousness prevails during ordinary self-conscious awareness when one is not meditating, incidents of cosmic consciousness can occur, resulting in vivid awareness of oneness or wholeness. The varied manifestations of life are then apprehended as being expressions of a single, unified reality. Because of increasingly clear states of consciousness that unfold, one more quickly awakens from illusions—from misperceptions that cause mental confusion—and from mental transformations which would ordinarily interfere with rational thinking and skillful use of intellectual powers. With the dawning of cosmic consciousness, insights into the reality of God and realizations of God naturally unfold. As Self-realization becomes more pronounced, so does realization that one's essential nature is an expression of God's consciousness become more vivid. This can occur gradually, or it can happen suddenly. While patiently undergoing transformative growth episodes on the spiritual path, it is also helpful to be open to the possibility of instantaneous illumination of consciousness. Our spiritual growth is not entirely due to our personal efforts. Our sincere desire for spiritual growth, our readiness for spiritual growth that we may not be consciously aware of, and the actions of grace can be influential.

3

The Life-Enhancing Benefits
of Contemplative Meditation
and Intentional Living

TO CONTEMPLATE IS TO LOOK AT, to examine, to
meditate upon something for the purpose of discovery.
When concentration progresses to undisturbed meditation, and meditation results in awakening which provides
insight, one's practice of contemplative meditation is
accomplished or successful. For this process to be facilitated the meditator needs to be alert and attentive.
Partially conscious or passive participation in meditation
practice will not be effective in producing satisfactory
results.

Until well into the 20th century, most people interested in learning about the effects of meditation had to
rely upon their own experiential endeavors or evaluate
anecdotal accounts professed by others who claimed
knowledge of the subject. Personal experience is, of course,
the best teacher, but it requires time and careful analysis
of what is experienced or apprehended. The shared accounts of others may, or may not, be trustworthy even
when sincerely proclaimed. Thankfully, for the past several decades, scientific research with volunteer medita-

tors has revealed that contemplative meditation, properly and regularly practiced, does confer many life-enhancing benefits—some of which I describe in this chapter.

Keep in mind that personal response to meditation and the beneficial unfoldments which can be actualized are almost always more immediate and satisfying when meditation practice is included in a balanced program of conscious, intentional living. Ever alert to the importance of being purposeful, all of our endeavors should be chosen with knowledge of why we implement them. Actions will then be chosen which are essential to our purposes, and actions which are not, can be disregarded. This approach greatly simplifies our lives, providing opportunities for personal fulfillment and spiritual enrichment in the most efficient manner.

Contemplative Meditation Provides
Deep, Conscious Rest and Renewal

As meditation progresses, breathing becomes slower and more refined, and tranquil calm becomes the prevailing mental condition, providing the meditator deeper, conscious rest and renewal than usually occurs during ordinary sleep. The body's life forces become balanced, contributing to organized function of physical systems.

Because of physical disturbance, emotional distress, or irregular sleep habits, many people do not get the rest they need when they sleep. The results may be low energy reserves, moodiness or depression, irritability, mental confusion, poor concentration, inefficient work performance, accident-prone behavior, and lower resistance to disease or illness. Meditation does not replace sleep, but one or two short meditation sessions a day will enliven the body, energize the mind, and contribute to improved performance of activities so that regular hours of sleep can be an interlude of undisturbed rest that is physically and mentally restorative.

As meditation results in the unfoldment of superconscious states which persist even during normal waking hours, one's regular hours of sleep may be occasioned by episodes of being conscious while the body and mind rests. The gaps between levels of consciousness become less defined and one may experience lucid perceptions of "being conscious of being conscious" during sleep, and of abiding in the *eternal now,* while simultaneously being aware of infinite oneness.

Contemplative Meditation Reduces Stress and Its Debilitating Effects

Because of deep relaxation and the physiological and psychological changes that occur during meditation, physical tension and mental anxiety fade as stress is reduced. An examination of blood lactate levels before and after meditation often reveals a reduction of those levels, which are usually higher when one is in a "fight or flight" physical and psychological state—a common condition for many people who feel it necessary to struggle to survive or who perceive threats to their well-being from real or imagined sources.

Even if one is not presently interested in spiritual growth, meditation practiced for twenty or thirty minutes once or twice a day for the stress-reducing effects, will greatly improve mental attitude and physical function and make it easier to accomplish purposes and to enjoy life more. The life-suppressing effects of hypertension are well documented. Common symptoms are high blood pressure, migraine headaches, and interference with normal functioning of physical systems. These symptoms often vanish once a regular meditation routine has been established. Do not make the mistake of falsely assuming meditation practice to be a cure-all. If the services of a health care professional are needed, by all means avail yourself of qualified assistance. When possible, you might want to seek out a health care person who has a holistic orientation and who will understand your interest and participation in self-responsible wellness regimens and spiritual growth practices.

Behavior related to biochemical influences is more actively being investigated at research centers around the world. Some fairly recent discoveries indicate that certain genetic defects can cause abnormal levels of serotonin and noradrenaline which, in turn, can influence human behaviors. Originating in the midbrain, these chemicals, referred to as neurotransmitters, enable cells in other parts of the brain to "talk" to each other by carrying messages between cells.

Serotonin, the brain's master impulse modulator for all emotions and drives, especially helps control aggression. Noradrenaline is the alarm hormone, triggered when danger to oneself is recognized or perceived as real, and organizes the brain to respond by signaling the production of adrenaline and other chemicals. When serotonin levels are lowered and noradrenaline levels are elevated in susceptible people exposed to environmental stresses, such as violent circumstances and alcohol use, a tendency toward violent activity may result. Low levels of serotonin are believed to be related to depression, suicidal impulses, impulsive aggression, addictive behaviors, sexual deviance, and episodes of sudden rage. High levels appear to be related to shyness, obsessive compulsive behavior, fearfulness, lack of self-confidence, and subdued levels of assertiveness. Low levels of noradrenaline are believed to be related to increased tendency toward premeditated acts of violence or thrill-seeking, while high levels may be related to overarousal of emotions, a tendency toward impulsive behaviors, passionate acts of violence, and rapid heartbeat.

These discoveries can provide some insight into human behavior. We must also remember that we are more than physical creatures: we are Spirit-mind-body events occurring in space-time. We cannot deny the effects of brain chemistry and hormonal influences upon our physiology and emotions when we are body-mind identified, for we have all experienced them. We should know, however, that there are ways to restore the body to a state of balance: by self-determined adjustment of mental attitude, moods, and behaviors; by choosing a food plan most suitable for our basic constitution; and by adhering to a sensible program of exercise, rest, intentional living, and spiritual practices.

A purely physical approach to behavior modification too often proceeds from a limited self-view that contributes to our believing that we are primarily effects of body

chemistry and environmental circumstances and conditions. When we choose to be more conscious and knowledgeable, we can discover that Spirit is superior to mind
and body, that mental and physical conditions can be
adjusted and organized, and that choices can be made in
relationship to behaviors which can beneficially influence
body chemistry and restore it to balance. Meditation can
be a foundation practice that enhances spiritual awareness, directly influences mind and body in entirely
constructive ways, and empowers us to knowledgeable,
Self-determined actions.

Strengthening the Body's Systems to Maintain Radiant Wellness

Stress, confusion, despair, anxiety, fear, loneliness,
hopelessness, unnatural living habits, and unhealthy
environmental conditions can weaken the body's immune
system, its safeguard against disease and deterioration.
Regular practice of contemplative meditation unfolds
superconscious states which, being superior to conditioned
states of consciousness, organize the body's systems and
infuse them with enlivening forces.

Intentional cultivation of optimism, hope, faith, pur-
posefulness, and feelings of love, also exercise a healthy,
nourishing influence upon the immune system. It is not
mere coincidence that happy, healthy-minded, creatively
purposeful people, are relatively disease-free and tend to
live longer, more successful lives. They know, consciously
or instinctively, that life is for living and respond with
enthusiasn to their opportunities to creatively express.

When internal fires, the body's metabolic forces, are most efficient, food transformation also occurs as designed by nature: producing plasma, blood, muscle, fat, bone, bone marrow, and reproductive essences. The final food transformation result is the production of a refined consciousness-energy essence that contributes to inner radiance and abundant energy: two obvious indications of vital wellness.

Contemplative meditation that results in sustained superconscious episodes regulates biochemical secretions and infuses the body with superior energy-frequencies which spiritualize it. Long-term meditators tend to experience a diminishment of biological aging processes. They have higher energy levels, keen interest in living, faster reactions to stimuli, usually better eyesight and hearing, and stronger immune systems than do persons who are not long-term meditators. Their biological ages are several years younger than their calendar years. When sixty years or older, their biological condition is ten, twenty, or more years younger.

From a material point of view, aging occurs because of genetic predisposition and the body's renewal processes being unable to keep up with the stresses and changes inflicted upon it. From a metaphysical perspective, aging occurs because the spiritual Self, the soul or essential Being, has forgotten its true nature and become overly identified with material processes and their actions and effects. As a result, instead of experiencing continual renewal, one dramatizes a fated, dying life.

The body is sustained by nature's forces which nurture it and soul forces which infuse it. When we are in harmony with natural forces and are spiritually awake, our bodies are effectively nurtured to become responsive instruments through which our enlightened purposes can be efficiently fulfilled. Healthy, long life has value in that it allows us to accomplish our major purposes, including that of Self-realization, in the present incarnation. This ideal may have little meaning to persons who are spiritually unawake, but holds much promise for all who are endowed with higher visions of possibilities.

Facilitating Rational Thinking,
Improved Powers of Concentration,
and Superior Intellectual Performance

When superconscious influences prevail during meditation, mental transformations become ordered. The chaos of conflicting thought streams, supported by emotional unrest and instinctual drives, ceases. During, and after, meditation one experiences expanded awareness and becomes capable of more rational thinking. Delusions (erroneous beliefs) and illusions (misperceptions) are either transcended or can be easily recognized and dismissed. The result is rational, coherent thinking: self-evident proof of sanity.

During meditation, so long as thinking persists, rationality enables the meditator to proceed with intentional precision. After meditation, one is enabled to process concepts and perceptions more skillfully, therefore, better able to live with intentional purpose and to implement actions which are appropriate and effective.

Concentration, intentional flowing of attention to the

object of attention, is vastly improved by meditation practice and facilitated by rational thinking at other times. Mental confusion and emotional conflicts become minimized when thought transformations become organized and physical well-being is maintained. Soul awareness is then unobstructed and can flow freely. With improved powers of concentration, contemplative meditation practice becomes more effective and functional living becomes more successful.

The power of intellectual determination is a spiritual ability demonstrated by using mental faculties. Beyond intellectual determination is intuitive perception: direct apprehension and comprehension of whatever is examined. Intuition is not dependent upon mental processes since it is the soul's capacity to know directly by knowing. When mental delusions and illusions prevail, or if the brain or nervous system is impaired, intellectual powers can be diminished. They can be improved by cultivating overall wellness, by rational thinking, and by introducing the mind and physiology to the enlivening, regenerative influences of higher states of consciousness. Superconscious influences, experienced during meditation and persisting afterward, enliven the nervous system, refine the brain structure, and purify the mental field: all of which contribute to allowing innate powers of intelligence to be more easily expressed.

Becoming More Self-Sufficient and
Creatively Functional by Unfolding
Your Innate Spiritual Potential

A healthy-minded person is, by nature, a problem-solver and goal-achiever. With awakened spiritual consciousness and the removal of inner restricting conditions, meditators can discover their innate potential and learn to flawlessly express it.

Meditation practice removes our awareness from limiting conditions, enabling us to acknowledge and experience ourselves as spiritual beings independent of relative circumstances. We become enabled to view ourselves in relationship to the universe from a higher perspective, to choose our thoughts and actions, and to flow with the rhythms of life with natural ease. Meditators can learn to *prosper*: to thrive, to flourish, and to be successful in all aspects of their lives.

At the level of soul awareness we are truly Self-sufficient because of knowing ourselves to be free souls, grounded in the unbounded field of Supreme Consciousness. The key to Self-sufficiency is to remain centered in Self-realization while performing all actions. Then, not only are our actions precisely appropriate for the occasion, we also experience a supportive relationship with the universe and demonstrate in our lives that the universe provides for us when we are in harmony with it.

All binding attachments, addictions, dependencies, and conditions which were once obstacles to creative living—including self-defeating attitudes, behaviors and relationships—disappear with our awakening to subjective knowledge and the emergence of clear understanding. Contemplative meditation provides the ideal opportunity to remove awareness from restricting circumstances so that conscious experience of Self-sufficiency can be actualized. My purpose in explaining these matters is to encourage the reader to be a completely functional person and to awaken from all restrictions and live freely. I want to awaken you to your innate immortality so that you can be consciously anchored in the Infinite.

Only the habit of mind-body identification keeps us from awareness of omnipresence. We are, as spiritual beings, as omnipresent as God is omnipresent. Omnipresence can be reclaimed by contemplative meditation and spontaneous episodes of cosmic consciousness which may unfold at any time. Every soul eventually has awareness restored to absolute freedom because of the innate urge to realize it, and the contributing influences of evolution and grace. When we cooperate with the spiritual growth process, our unfoldment is more rapid and enjoyable. Dedicated meditation practice and conscious, intentional living is the proven way to realize illumination of mind and consciousness and to fulfill soul destiny.

To actualize our soul capacities and express life's fullness we have to be open and responsive to our available good. We demonstrate our openness by our willing participation. The following story* by Rabindranath Tagore serves as an illustrative reminder of our need to do this:

I had gone a-begging from door to door in the village path, when thy golden chariot appeared in the dis-

* *Gitanjali: A Collection of Indian Songs*, circa 1913.

tance like a gorgeous dream and I wondered who was this King of kings!

My hopes rose high and methought my evil ways were at an end, and I stood waiting for alms to be given unasked and for wealth to be scattered on all sides in the dust.

The chariot stopped where I stood. Thy glance fell on me and thou camest down with a smile. I felt that the luck of my life had come at last. Then of a sudden thou didst hold out thy right hand and say, "What hast thou to give to me?"

Ah, what kingly jest it was to open thy palm to a begger to beg! I was confused and stood undecided, and then from my wallet I slowly took out the least little grain of corn and gave it to thee.

But how great was my surprise when at the day's end I emptied my bag on the floor to find a least little grain of gold among the poor heap. I bitterly wept and wished that I had had the heart to give thee my all.

Part Two

How to Meditate
for Personal Fulfillment
and Spiritual Growth

The soul, when it shall have driven away from itself all that is contrary to the Divine Will, becomes transformed in love—the soul then becomes immediately enlightened by and transformed in God.

Saint John of Cross (16th century)

Human beings naturally feel the necessity to experience the truth of themselves: existence, unobstructed awareness, and the sheer joy of Self-knowledge. These have nothing to do with anything outside the Self or soul. They are innate characteristics of one's real nature.

Sri Yukteswar

He that dwells in the secret place of the most High shall abide under the shadow of the Almighty.

Book of Psalms 91:1

4

The Procedure

STEADY FLOWING OF ATTENTION to the field of unmodified Existence-Being is the purest, most direct form of meditation. Behind our thoughts and emotions, this field exists as self-complete wholeness. Any preliminary procedure that enables us to remove awareness from distractions and awaken to transcendental realities is a useful meditation practice.

The ideal procedure is one which enables the meditator to accomplish the purpose of practice efficiently and quickly. The aim of procedure is to clear the mental field of the transformations and changes which ordinarily persist during states of consciousness other than when the most refined states of superconsciousness prevail.

The only prerequisites for practicing meditation are sincere interest, sufficient intelligence to understand the procedure, ability to follow recommended guidelines, and willingness to practice. The procedure can be learned in less than an hour; acquiring proficiency will require as much time as necessary for the purpose of practice to be accomplished. Progress will be slow, moderate, or rapid, depending upon one's intention, participation, and the transformational changes which have to occur to allow innate knowledge and awareness to unfold or be Self-revealed. The important matter is to learn how to proceed, then begin. Nothing useful will be accomplished without purposeful endeavor.

There is only one way to enlightenment—to total, conscious realization of our real nature, God, and universal processes—and that is to awaken from simple consciousness to self-consciousness, superconsciousness, cosmic consciousness, God-consciousness, and transcendental consciousness. Procedures used to enable us to live in harmony with natural forces and to make ourselves responsive to spiritual growth impulses are universally applicable: they are basic, and suitable for all people regardless of who they are or what their outer circumstances might be. It is recommended that one who is sincerely interested in spiritual growth make an honest effort to live a self-responsible, moral, healthy life, as this will ensure harmony with the environment, contribute to psychological and physical wellness, and provide a firm foundation from which to proceed to spiritual growth. For this reason all enlightenment traditions have guidelines to this end. While they may be described in different ways, they are essentially the same in emphasis.

One who is sincere and intentional on the spiritual growth path is advised to be compassionate and harmless in relationships; to be truthful; honest; wise in the use of vital powers; and to be responsible in actions and successful in endeavors, while avoiding egocentric attitudes and attachments to persons, things, circumstances, or the results of personal actions. These are the behaviors to actualize in regard to relationships, to ensure harmony with the natural order and to maintain inner peace. The internal disciplines include purity of attitude and intention; contentment in all circumstances so that soul peace is never disturbed; necessary self-analysis and attitudinal and behavioral changes which can contribute to psychological transformation (to rid one of all conflicts and mental and emotional restrictions to the actualization of soul awareness); profound study of the natural sciences (in order to live in right relationship with the world and function successfully in it) and metaphysical principles (to acquire understanding of the nature of consciousness, God, soul, and spiritual growth processes); and to trust in, and surrender to, evolutionary processes and God's grace. These guidelines are emphasized in the major religious and philosophical writings of many cultures.

There are six stages through which we unfold during meditation practice, which may be experienced sequentially or may be moved through almost instantaneously: settled meditation posture, harmonizing of the body's life forces, internalization of attention, concentration, pure meditation, and the peak experience or realization. To facilitate meditation practice, these stages should be understood and knowledge of how to move through them should be acquired and applied.

1. *Settled Meditation Posture* – The ideal posture for meditation practice is an upright, seated position which is comfortable and relaxed and allows contemplation to proceed without physical distractions. One may sit on a chair or wherever convenient. A seated, cross-legged pos-

ture is suitable, if comfortable. When first sitting, be alert, with attention flowing into the area between the eyebrows and the higher brain.

2. *Harmonizing the Body's Life Forces* – If devotional ardor is impelling and inward flowing of attention occurs immediately, the body's vital forces will be regulated naturally, relaxation will become deeper, and meditation will proceed smoothly. If this does not happen right away, there are techniques which can be used which will be helpful in harmonizing life forces and inducing physical relaxation and mental calm.

3. *Internalization of Attention* – When attention is successfully withdrawn from environmental and physical circumstances and turned back to the higher brain centers, internalization occurs, allowing concentration and contemplation to be easily experienced. Mental transformations and mood swings may continue for a duration, but these will be quieted and transcended as meditation progresses.

4. *Steady Concentration* – Concentration is steady when attention flows without interruption to the focus of contemplation. The procedures described in this book can be used with benefit to maintain concentration while avoiding involvement with random thought processes and emotional states.

5. *Pure Meditation* – When concentration flows effortlessly to the focus of contemplation, pure meditation is

experienced. All that occurs prior to this is preliminary and preparatory. Now meditation is being perfectly experienced and results will spontaneously follow.

6. *The Peak Experience* – Upon awakening to the clearest level of awareness possible during the meditation episode—which is the peak experience for that session—one should remain in it for as long it is comfortable and compelling. This is the stage during which highest benefits are actualized. The deep relaxation and mental calm influence mind and body in constructive ways. While being surrendered to the experience, be open to the possibility of spontaneous unfoldments which can occur, but do not strain to cause anything to happen.

If you are one of the fortunate few who experience spontaneous meditation when you turn your attention to the process, you need not use meditation techniques except for special occasions when meditation does not occur easily. Meditation techniques are practical tools to use when needed. When the purpose of using a meditation technique has been served, it can be discarded.

If you have a religious orientation, prayer can be a direct approach to meditation practice. For this, simply and sincerely pray to God as you feel led from your heart. Pray for spiritual awakening, for realization of yourself as a spiritual being, and for knowledge and experience of God. Pray until prayer ceases, then be still and let meditation unfold.

Whatever your approach to meditation, have no anxiety about the outcome. Anxiety causes stress, which

interferes with the meditation process. Use any preliminary process you find helpful to internalize your attention, then let the results happen naturally. Let your
ego—your sense of individual selfhood—dissolve. Do not
carry your ego-demands into the meditation process. If
you do, you may be inclined to try to force results. You
may create an altered mental state which may be falsely
assumed to be a superconscious state or indulge in creating feelings or moods to create a condition of artificial
happiness. For soul awareness to be authentic it must be
allowed to unfold. Any created mental or emotional state
is not true spiritual awareness, but only a condition produced by personal endeavor or imagination. Superconsciousness, soul awareness, is outside the range of
mind and emotions. Whether using prayer or any other
technique as your approach to meditation, use the technique to remove attention and awareness from physical
and mental processes, then renounce personal effort and
contemplate higher possibilities with an attitude of gentle
anticipation and watchfulness, allowing unfoldments to
occur naturally and spontaneously.

Another practice, to be used when you first sit or whenever you need to collect your thoughts and center yourself, is that of watching the natural flow of breathing. For
this, be still and let the body breathe. Experience the
actions of breathing while observing the process. Doing
this can induce relaxation as well as easily remove your
attention from involvements with outer conditions and
mental and emotional states. When you are somewhat
calm and centered, proceed with meditation.

*Mantra Meditation: the Procedure
and the Results of Right Practice*

One of the easiest meditation techniques to use which is suitable for anyone, is mantra. This Sanskrit word is derived from *manas,* thinking principle, and *tra,* that which protects the mind and takes awareness beyond it. A meditation mantra is a sound which serves as an attractive focus of attention during preliminary stages of meditation practice. It may be a meaningless word, a word which has a meaning which may contemplated as the sound is listened to, or a sound which arises within one's field of awareness.

The usefulness of mantra contemplation is that the meditator's attention becomes so involved with it that awareness of physical and mental activities is replaced by awareness of the mantra; thus solving the major problem that many meditators encounter—that of overcoming preoccupation with feelings and thought processes.

For the purpose of inducing relaxation and creating favorable psychological states, one may use any pleasant word or word-phrase as the meditation mantra. This can be self-chosen or it may be recommended by one's spiritual mentor or a qualified meditation teacher. One should feel comfortable with the mantra if its use during meditation practice is to be satisfying. Words commonly used as meditation mantras include *God, peace, joy, light, love, Om,* and others that have meaning to the meditator or which agreeably serve the purpose of practice. Word-phrases may be used, so long as it is understood that they are not to be considered as affirmations for conditioning the mind, but are merely statements of ideal states of awareness to be consciously unfolded and actualized. Word phrases may be, "I am one with God," "I am peace.... love...light...(or any other quality or attribute of higher significance)." The thing to remember is that the meditation mantra is attractive to the mind and so involves the meditator's attention that adjustments to clear states of consciousness can be more easily facilitated.

Sanskrit meditation mantras are believed to have the added, beneficial influences of the energy-frequencies of their sounds, which have a calming effect on the mind and enliven the nervous system. Common Sanskrit mantras are *hong-sau* (pronounced as "hong-saw"), *so-ham,* and others, as single words or word combinations. These are best learned from a qualified meditation teacher, to learn the sounds of the words and how to use them as mantras. When given during initiation into meditation practice, mantras can also be infused with the qualities of the spiritual energies which are present during the occasion of initiation.

All Sanskrit mantras derive their potency from the *Word* (Aum, Om), the primal sound current from which the universes are manifested. When meditating with such mantras, one is encouraged to remember the source of all expressive sounds—which is the Word or Om—and that Om originates in the field of the Godhead. One can then merge in the mantra and go beyond it to transcendental perceptions and realizations. Listening to the mantra calms the mind and improves concentration. For best results, the ideal is to eventually transcend the mantra, for it, too, is but a technique or tool to be used to facilitate meditation practice.

When a mantra is used, it is introduced into one's field of awareness, usually as a mental sound. It may be mentally affirmed at the beginning, then mentally "listened to" as though resonating within one's mind and field of awareness. The key to mantra practice is to give full attention to the inner sound, while remaining relaxed and attentive. Mantras are sometimes mentally listened to in conjunction with being aware of the body's breathing rhythm. When this is done, it is usually experienced during the early stages of meditation practice, until one is sufficiently relaxed and internalized to ignore the breath and give full attention to the mantra and to possibilities of experiencing superconscious states. Variations of meditation technique practices can be learned from a teacher or by personal experimentation.

Meditators whose primary interest is to experience relaxation and mental calm usually practice meditation, whether with mantra or some other approach, until they experience a stable, tranquil state of consciousness, then rest in it for a duration. Meditators whose aspiration is higher, will consider this stage as but the starting point for deeper contemplation leading to more profound superconscious unfoldments and insights. Therefore, contemplative meditation is suitable for anyone, regardless of the need or desire for life-enhancement or for more satisfying spiritual growth. Its faithful practice will take one as deep into knowledge and experience of life as aspiration impels.

In the early stages of meditation, the mental calm that is experienced provides the mind with a superior, satisfying pleasure which it finds attractive and desires to return to whenever possible. One then notices that scheduled meditation sessions are eagerly anticipated because of the enjoyment that results from practice. In this way, the mind's instinctive pleasure-seeking inclination is used to advantage. Repeated successful meditation episodes attract the mind to the experience of refined pleasure to such an extent that many of the addictions and attachments which, perhaps were once sought, are no longer as attractive to it. This, and the increased sense of Self-fulfillment that results from meditation practice, makes it easier for a meditator to choose to avoid actions and circumstances which are perceived as not being conducive to wellness and successful living. It is the testimony of many persons who have been meditating for only a few days or weeks, to report that their values have changed and they find it easier to choose lifestyle behaviors which are more constructive.

The Usefulness of Keeping the Procedure Simple

Remembering that the purpose of meditation practice is to allow unfoldment of superconscious states, we are wise to adhere to the basics and avoid preoccupation with matters which cannot be supportive of our highest aspirations. Whatever we do, when involved in the meditation process, is to facilitate relaxation, calmness, and spiritual awakening. Anything we think or do that contributes to stress, mental confusion, emotional conflict, or illusions of any kind, is not in our best interest and should be renounced. Once one knows how to meditate, what should then follow is a consistent schedule of regular practice. Just as anxiety about results should be avoided when meditating, so there should be no anxiety about results after meditation. It is all right to be aware of the fact that the most recent meditation session was enjoyable and beneficial, or to be aware that improvement in practice is needed, but it is not helpful to overly analyze meditation experiences. Also not recommended is discussion with others about one's meditation experiences. Our inner growth is a personal matter and our growing relationship with the Infinite is subtle and intimate, and neither should be taken lightly or subjected to the opinions of others who do not apprehend our intentions.

With the same attentiveness we devote to spiritual practices, we should devote to our everyday relationships, duties, and chosen activities. This will ensure balance between inner and outer, subjective and objective, aspects of life. To become disinterested in the secular world while we still have responsibilities and learning opportunities in it, is to be impractical and restricts emotional, intellectual, and spiritual growth. Just as obsessive preoccupation with worldly concerns is spiritually limiting, so obsession with "spiritual matters" is symptomatic of emotional immaturity. A balanced life is best, allowing for the cultivation of intellectual and spiritual growth and for fulfilling duties and purposes in the most practical ways. We can be happy and successful in this world while continuing to unfold our innate potential.

5

How to Practice Meditation

BY DEDICATED PRACTICE of meditation you will provide for yourself ideal opportunities for experiencing personal benefits and spiritual growth. At all times, when meditating and when engaged in daily routines, cultivate awareness of yourself as a spiritual being with unlimited potential, instead of seeing and feeling yourself to be a mere human creature. You will then know your spiritual practices to be for the purpose of facilitating your awakening to knowledge and realization of your real nature. To ensure successful results, do the following:

1. *Commit to Regular Practice* – Firmly resolve that you will meditate on a regular schedule. Consider your meditation session as your daily appointment with the Infinite and keep that appointment without fail. Should you, for one reason or another, have to miss your practice session, do not punish yourself with feelings of guilt or regret. Just make the most of every available opportunity.

Choose a time that will be most ideal for your practice. If you meditate twice a day, early morning and in the late afternoon or evening are suitable times. Early morning meditation will prepare you for the day's activities, and late afternoon or evening practice will enable you to relax and experience renewal after the day's work or activity. If you meditate once a day, choose a time when you are most alert and able to give yourself fully to your practice. Early morning is a good time, but whenever you decide is all right. Avoid regular practice sessions immediately after eating or when overly tired, as these will not be the best circumstances to support alert concentration.

Choose a place that is comfortable and quiet, where you will not be disturbed. Any quiet place will do. If can arrange a special place to be used for your spiritual practices, so much the better. If you do this, let it be your private sanctuary, to be used only for prayer, meditation, and contemplative reflection. You will then associate your special place with that purpose and immediately become more soul centered when you go there. Have a comfortable chair on which to sit. If necessary, turn off the telephone. You have transcendental interests to attend to, so eliminate the possibility of any secular intrusion when you settle down to meditate.

Approach your practice session with keen interest. Have a specific meditation routine in mind before you start to meditate. If you are a new meditator (or are a regular meditator and want to experiment with a new procedure) use the following routine to your benefit:

2. *Sit Upright and Be Comfortable* – Sit in a relaxed, upright posture with your head erect. Meditation is a conscious, intentional practice, so enter into it with full

attention. Let your breathing flow naturally. With your
eyes closed, look into the space between your eyebrows,
without straining to do so. Let your awareness include
the spinal pathway and higher brain. Withdraw your
attention from the body into the spinal pathway and upward to the spiritual eye center between your eyebrows.
Doing this begins the internalizing process.

3. *Open Yourself to the Infinite* – Feel your ego boundaries dissolving. Be happy. Feel thankful for the gift of
life and for the opportunity to expand your consciousness.
If you want to pray to God, now is the time to do so, to
invoke an awareness of God's presence. However God is
real to you—or however you think of yourself in relationship to God—open your heart, your Being, to God. Just
follow your guidance on this. There is no need to rush the
process. It may be that you will immediately begin to flow
into meditation. If this happens, go along with it, letting
your innate intelligence direct the process. If the meditation process does not begin to flow, move to the next stage.

4. *Practice Your Preferred Meditation Technique* – If
you already have a mantra or a meditation technique that
serves you well, use it now. Otherwise, experiment with
mantra. Whatever word, word-phrase, or sound you have
chosen for your practice, introduce it into your field of
awareness and listen to it. Let your attention become fully
engaged. Within a few minutes, you will no longer be
aware of physical restlessness or discomfort, or of moods
or random thoughts: you will be absorbed in the mantra.
Remain alert and watchful even as you participate in the

process. Avoid passivity, sleepiness, or daydreaming. Be alert and attentive, while relaxed and surrendered to meditation. Continue until you experience what seems to you to be the peak phase of practice, during which you are peaceful and soul content. Rest at this phase, letting the deep peace beneficially influence your mind and body. If you are meditating for the psychological and physiological benefits only, or for rest and renewal, enjoy this level of tranquil calm until you feel inclined to conclude your practice.

If you are meditating for the purpose of experiencing higher superconscious states and for more profound contemplation of transcendental realities, after becoming stable at this phase of internalized peacefulness, go deeper.

5. *Concluding Your Practice* – When you feel inclined to conclude your practice, bring your awareness into relationship with your thoughts, feelings, and senses. Sit for a few moments to allow a smooth transition from inner focusing to outer acknowledgement of your environment. Then go about your usual routine, maintaining inner awareness of your spiritual nature and the calmness unfolded during meditation.

If you have special needs to examine, problems to solve, or decisions to make, a good time to give attention to such matters is during the conclusion of meditation practice, while you are still soul-centered, calm, and able to maintain an objective attitude.

This procedure can be used with benefit by anyone. The more you consciously practice, the more proficient

you will become. You will find that your innate urge to
have awareness restored to conscious realization of oneness will motivate and guide you during meditation practice and when you are engaged in the performance of
duties.

Especially if you are a new meditator, be patient, and
allow yourself time to learn about spiritual growth processes by personal experience. It is also a good idea to
avoid preoccupation with visions, or any other perceptions
or sensations which interfere with progressive unfoldments of soul awareness. Visions perceived during meditation are similar to dreams that occur during ordinary
sleep, and are symptoms of emotional discontent and
mental restlessness. While meditation can be an enjoyable experience, the purpose of meditation is not to
create a pleasant emotional state and become attached to
it. Enjoy meditation practice, remembering that the aim
is higher knowledge along with Self-realization, not continued involvement with minor ecstasies. Whatever is
experienced or perceived, if it is subject to change, is not
the ultimate realization we aspire to actualize. Whenever
tempted to become attached to meditation perceptions,
ask yourself, "Who is experiencing this?" You will then be
reminded that you are the experiencer and the observer,
therefore, superior to what is perceived. Desire to know
your true nature as a spiritual being independent of
objects of perception. Be inspired to full illumination of
consciousness by reading the following words attributed
to Sri Krishna by the author of the *Bhagavad Gita.*
Krishna, speaking to his disciple Arjuna, advises him on
the ideal approach to meditation practice for the purpose

of realizing oneness (yoga):

> Let the practitioner of yoga constantly concentrate attention on the Supreme Reality, remaining in solitude and alone, free from desires and longings for possessions or sense experience. Having the body positioned in a firm posture, making his attention one-pointed, controlling thoughts and senses, let him practice pure concentration in order to attain inward purity. Holding body, head, and neck erect and still, flowing awareness to the spiritual eye without allowing his eyes to wander, serene and fearless, firm in his vow of self-control, subdued in mind, let him sit harmonized, contemplating the field of Pure Consciousness which is the single Reality. The devoted meditator of controlled mind, ever remaining harmonized, attains to transcendental peace, the supreme realization.

Awakening Through the Levels of Progressive Spiritual Growth

Because of the soul's inclination to unfold its potential, spiritual growth occurs whenever conditions are suitable for expression. You can learn to recognize the signs of your own spiritual growth by self-observation, and experience progressive awakenings during contemplative meditation. By learning to cooperate with our innate inclination to unfold awareness and knowledge, our spiritual growth can be more rapid.

Some signs of natural spiritual growth are emotional maturity, optimism, selflessness, compassionate feelings and actions, faith, trust in God, improved sense of meaningful purpose, mental poise, keen intellectual powers, awakened intuition, generosity, love of truth, and an increasing awareness of life's wholeness. These are but a few indications of awakened spiritual consciousness.

During meditation, adjustments of states of consciousness can be observed and experienced. With physical relaxation and internalization of attention, as mental transformations become refined, so our states of consciousness become refined. We can notice this by observing changes as they occur. Once we know what subtle and refined levels of consciousness feel like, and what our awareness is at these levels, we can choose to shift awareness to preferred levels at will without having to initiate physical or mental actions to facilitate change.

When meditation practice removes our awareness from physical and mental involvements, and we remain alert, superconsciousness can emerge. Preliminary superconsciousness may be experienced while emotions and thought processes are somewhat influential. When emotions and thought processes are stilled, pure superconscious states can unfold. Preliminary, thoughtless superconsciousness may result in tranquil states which are enjoyable. As soul potential unfolds spontaneously, or because of intentional contemplation of transcendental realities, superconsciousness can result in episodes of expanded awareness or cosmic consciousness, which is attended by apprehension of realities impossible to perceive or experience through the senses. Self-knowledge or Self-realization occurs. Then God-knowledge and realization unfolds. From here, further unfoldments are due to the actions of grace.

Yearning for full illumination is a powerful aid to remaining focused on the spiritual path. Without intense desire for illumination of consciousness it can be easy to go off course, to be tempted to settle for less than what is possible, or to become sidetracked because of being fascinated with perceptions of relative phenomena. One may experience authentic spiritual growth to a certain stage of unfoldment and falsely assume that the goal has been attained. Or one may become smugly self-righteous because of partial attainment. I have known many "devotees of God" whose ability to experience preliminary levels of superconsciousness was obvious, yet who, for years, continued to dramatize self-serving behaviors and attitudes which indicated their lack of emotional and spiritual maturity. They may have acquired a considerable degree of functional ability and could meditate and experience tranquil mental states, but were not inspired to transcend their limitations. They have made the spiritual path their abode, instead of going beyond it to full mental illumination and liberation of consciousness.

When meditating, remain focused on the ideal of awakening to the clearest levels of consciousness you are capable of experiencing. If thoughts intrude, ignore or dismiss them. You are not mind, therefore, you are not thoughts. When you are highly motivated, and devoted to your meditation ideal, it will be easy to avoid involvements with thoughts and moods. Mental transformations and mood changes will occur as long as restlessness causes impulses to arise from unconscious levels of the mind. These impulses cause movements in the mental field that flow like waves.

When your concentration improves and your body becomes relaxed, impulses caused by restlessness become diminished in intensity, thoughts become more refined, and the mental field becomes increasingly clear. Note that mental activity is not suppressed by meditation. Instead, the calming effects of meditation result in a natural quieting of impulses that ordinarily cause disorganized mental activity. With mental calm, superconscious states become more pronounced.

If, when meditating, you feel energy surges that tend to cause body movement, remain poised and still, as physical reaction will interfere with the flow of meditation. Relax more completely, directing the energy flows from the spinal pathway into the spiritual eye and higher brain. By doing this your meditation experience will be improved.

If you perceive inner light while meditating, determine its cause. If you become aware that you are drifting into a twilight sleep state, avoid it by choosing to be more alert. If light perception is due to electrical stimulation of the optic nerves and the inner light remains steady, you can use it to keep your attention internalized just as you use your mantra to keep your attention flowing inward. If inner light is not perceived, proceed without it. You, as an individualized unit of God's consciousness, are superior to whatever you perceive.

Likewise, if you become aware of subtle sounds resonating in your ears, you can use them as a mantra: listening to them, merging somewhat in them, and contemplating the field of unmanifest consciousness which is the origin of sound. In the following chapter are descriptions of light and sound perceptions that may be worked with for the purpose of deepening the meditation experience. These techniques are recommended for experienced meditators who are intent upon exploring subjective realms and are doing all they can to facilitate rapid spiritual growth. For persons presently interested only in psychological and physical benefits to be derived from meditation practice, advanced meditation techniques are not necessary. If you are an experienced meditator—or are moving in that direction—it is recommended that you adhere to basic routines as a foundation for more advanced practices.

Constantly be self-reminded that, while you adhere to a regular meditation practice routine, the time given to it represents only a modest portion of the day. It is during the remaining waking hours that you have an opportunity to continue your spiritual practices. You can choose to do this by remaining centered and calm, remembering that you are a spiritual being expressing through mind and body, while cultivating all of the desirable soul qualities and expressing them: seeing all people as spiritual beings and relating to them as such; living with meaningful purpose; and being always open to your highest good. It is when relating to everyday circumstances that we have moment-to-moment opportunities to demonstrate our understanding in practical ways. Doing this is just as important as introspective study and contemplative meditation. It is by living from our highest understanding that we affirm our spiritual growth and validate our knowledge. The only way to prove to ourselves what we know—or think we know—is to express it.

Innate soul abilities, which some people erroneously

refer to as supernatural powers, will unfold along with awakened spiritual consciousness. It is only natural that this should occur. Use them for selfless, constructive purposes just as you now use the knowledge and creative skills you have. It is not the demonstration of higher knowledge that interferes with spiritual growth—it is self-centered, purposeless, or misdirected use of knowledge and ability that complicates our lives and interferes with soul destiny.

Personal abilities, used solely for self-centered, materialistic purposes, keep us attached to the objective realm and blind us to subjective realities. We see examples of this in the lives of spiritually unawake people we meet every day or are informed about through various news media. Why do we awaken to higher knowledge if it is not to be expressed? It *is* to be expressed, but wisely. Awakening to awareness of our soul abilities is somewhat like becoming aware of the fact that we are truly rich after a long duration of poverty. It requires an adjustment of attitude, a shift from beliefs of limitation to knowledge of freedom, and from purposelessness to self-responsible behaviors.

Therefore, while aspiring to illumination of consciousness, pray for guidance so that you will know how to adapt to the radical changes that will occur in your life as a result of accelerated spiritual growth.

Part Three

Advanced Practices, Alternative Techniques, and Innovative Routines for Experienced Meditators

Reclaiming Omnipresence
Meditation to Expand Awareness

It is only habit that confines our awareness to the body and the limitations imposed by conditioned mental states. At the soul level, we are omnipresent (everywhere present) and omniscient (all knowing). Practice contemplative meditation to reclaim your awareness of omnipresence and omniscience.

Relax into meditation. At the spiritual eye, visualize a sphere of blue light. Merge in that light. Be that conscious, blue light.

As conscious, blue light, expand in all directions until you fill your body, then extend beyond it. Feel your body existing within your field of consciousness. Continue to expand as conscious, blue light until you fill the room in which your body resides. Continue to expand, to include the nearby community, Planet Earth, the solar system, and the galaxy with its billions of suns. Expand to include the galaxies. Feel the universe floating within your field of awareness.

Pierce the veils of matter to include astral realms, causal electric-magnetic realms, Cosmic Mind, the field of Primal Nature (Om, cosmic particles, space, and time). Feel yourself to be one with God. Contemplate the field of pure Existence-Being. Be open to discovery. Rejoice in omnipresence and omniscience.

Remain absorbed in cosmic contemplation until the process concludes by itself. Remember your omnipresence as you attend to routine duties and relationships.

6

Meditation Practice for Devotees of God

FOR SUPERIOR RESULTS, be more focused and intentional in your spiritual practices. Maintain a balance between inner work and outer activities with your spiritual practices as the foundation upon which all other actions are based. Surely, anyone who is sincerely interested in spiritual growth can set aside at least one hour a day for contemplative meditation practice. Don't let the excuse of "I'm too busy to do that" prevent you from choosing to make spiritual growth first in order of priorities in your daily schedule.

Review your activity schedule, retaining those duties and relationships which are of importance and value, and eliminating those which are not essential. Decide how much time and energy to use for self-improvement studies and spiritual practices. Then decide how much time and energy to allot for family and social interaction, work, charitable activities, leisure, sleep and other self-careroutines, and for whatever else you consider to be necessary or worthwhile. Discipline yourself so that you are able to easily accomplish everything with relative ease.

Let all you do be intentional and act so that outcomes of actions are entirely constructive. Put your attention, thoughts, feelings, actions, and resources where your heart is. Live not from your emotions but from your Being, from soul awareness. We can easily determine what is important to us by how we live: by what we choose to do with our energy, abilities, resources, and available time.

You need not be concerned about what others think. Maintain friendly, supportive relationships with people with whom you choose to share your life, while maintaining your spiritual integrity. Your spiritual growth practices are personal and private and it is to your advantage to keep them that way.

In an earlier chapter I suggested the usefulness of setting aside a special place for spiritual practices. For the intentional devotee of truth, I strongly recommend it. Not only will your special place ensure privacy and be a constant reminder of why you are there, it will become highly charged with refined energies as the result of your regular prayer and meditation experiences. When you go there, you will be mentally elevated and inspired with devotion to your high purpose. Keep your special place, your personal sanctuary, simple and clean. Have there only what is supportive of your practices; a comfortable place to sit and perhaps a modest centerpiece or altar with pictures of saints, or any other items that have spiritual significance for you. When you first prepare it for your private use, consecrate it with conscious intention to the purpose it serves. Whenever you go there, enter with a respectful attitude and immediately feel more open to the Infinite.

Helpful Guidelines for Committed
Devotees on the Spiritual Path

Acquire as much useful information about the spiritual path as possible. Turn to valid sources of knowledge, such as spiritually aware teachers and books written by people who have understanding. Learn about the nature of consciousness, God, the soul nature, and the universe. While doing this, use your intelligence and common sense to determine what is true and discard what is not. Ensure peace of mind by avoiding useless philosophical discussions. When true insight reveals the fallacy of beliefs, renounce them with thankfulness. Read a little, contemplate what you have learned until you understand it, meditate more, and apply what you truly know in practical ways. In the beginning, some philosophical explanations of higher realities may not be fully comprehended. As you grow spiritually, your innate knowledge will unfold and you will eventually understand everything.

One thing you should know, in order to meditate effectively, is how you are related to your mind and body. As a soul, a spiritual being identified with mind and matter, your life forces blend with your mind and body to energize and enliven them. The initial connection is at the medulla oblongata at the base of the brain. From there, life forces flow from the brain downward, and are distributed through vital centers along the spine and into the body. The Sanskrit word for these centers is *chakra*, which means "wheel." Descending life force (*prana*) changes in frequency-influence at each center to perform various functions in the subtle and physical bodies. For the meditator, two flows of prana are of interest: the descending flow which carries life force down the spinal pathway, and the ascending flow which reverses it back to the brain centers. During the early stages of meditation practice it is helpful to identify with the ascending flow and encourage its actions. This will induce life forces which are not needed to maintain ordinary biological function to be withdrawn to the spinal pathway and directed upward to the brain. This action effectively withdraws the meditator's attention from environmental conditions and sensory sensation, thus eliminating these as possible causes of distraction.

Three distinct flows of prana occur along the spinal pathway. The flow along the left side is referred to as the moon current. Its influence on mind and body is cooling and quieting. The flow along the right side is referred to as the sun current. Its influence on mind and body is heating and stimulating. When these flows are harmonized, prana flows are more influential through the central pathway. The Sanskrit word for this channel is *sushumna*: the pathway of God.

During the course of a twenty-four hour day, prana ordinarily flows with greater dominance through either the right or left spinal channel for approximately two hours, when one is in a healthy condition. Physical, emotional, or mental circumstances can change this rhythm. When the flow is dominant in the left channel, air flow is also dominant through the left nostril. When the flow is dominant in the right channel, air flow is also dominant through the right nostril. An interesting physiological condition is involved with this process. The nasal passages

have erectile tissue, which is also found in the breasts
and genital organs. When the current is flowing in the
left channel, the flow of air is dominant through the left
nostril because the right nostril is partially blocked by
the swollen tissue of the nasal pathway. The opposite
situation occurs when the current is flowing through the
right channel: the right nostril air flow is dominant because the left nasal pathway is partially blocked by swollen tissue.

When right nostril breathing is dominant and the sun
current is active, one tends to be more outgoing, goal
oriented, intellectually discerning, and inclined to make
decisions easily. When left nostril breathing is dominant,
one tends to be more introverted, imaginative, passive,
and inclined to indecision and fantasy. With right nostril
dominance, the left hemisphere of the brain is dominant.
With left nostril dominance, the right hemisphere of the
brain is dominant. When prana currents flow evenly
through both channels along the spine, air flows evenly
through both nostrils, contributing to balanced brain wave
activity. This is a useful condition for meditation practice.

If one enters immediately into meditation, prana flows
respond and tend to become harmonized regardless of their
actions prior to sitting for meditation. But if one is restless or too passive when first sitting to meditate, these
prana flows can be encouraged to balance out—with a corresponding balancing effect upon body and mind—by the
expedient practice of a basic *pranayama*, a breathing technique used to directly influence them. *Prana* means first
unit of life force, and *yama* means restraint. We can regu-

late flows of prana in the body by regulating the breathing pattern. In this instance, the approach is to practice alternate nostril breathing eight or ten times.

A good time to do this is just after sitting, and before starting your meditation routine. Proceed by placing your right hand at your nose with your thumb at the right nostril and a finger at the left nostril. Inhale a little more deeply than usual and exhale almost completely. Don't overdo it. Close the right nostril and inhale smoothly and completely through the left nostril. Pause for a moment. Close off the left nostril and exhale completely through the right nostril. Pause for a moment. Inhale through the right nostril. Pause. Exhale through the left nostril. That is one round. Do eight or ten rounds in this manner. Then breathe in through both nostrils and exhale naturally. Proceed with your usual meditation routine.

This practice balances the flows of prana through left and right channels and contributes to even air flows through both nostrils. Practice gently, without violent effort, breathing a little more deeply than usual but not excessively so. Find your own rhythm which is comfortable and relaxing.

If you are an established meditator and are able to practice easily and effectively for short sessions, it can be useful to extend your meditation session to forty-five minutes or an hour. This will provide more time for in-depth contemplation and experience. There is no need to struggle with the process. Be intentional, while going with the flow of meditation so that the experience is always enjoyable.

If you are already sitting for forty-five minutes to an hour and are comfortable doing this, now and then sit for another thirty minutes to an hour. Also, once a week or once a month, schedule a two or three hour session. If you are not comfortable with longer sessions and want to be more intentional in practice, include an extra meditation session during the day. If you meditate once a day, change to a twice a day schedule. If you meditate twice a day, change to a three times a day schedule for a week or more, to give yourself a chance to notice any positive changes.

If you find that you are becoming so preoccupied with subjective contemplation that you are losing interest in worthwhile relationships and duties, shorten your meditation time and get back into a balanced schedule of meditation and meaningful activity. Don't use meditation and contemplation as an excuse to withdraw from life or to avoid responsibilities and learning opportunities.

Alternative Meditation Techniques
to Learn and Use with Benefit

The following meditation techniques have been passed from guru to disciple, teacher to student, for centuries. They continue to be taught because they produce results. You do not have to be spiritually advanced to use them with benefit. Carefully read the instructions for practice and patiently experiment until you find them easy to use, then include them in your meditation routine. Keep in mind that techniques are only useful tools to be used to assist you to accomplish your purposes for meditation, and can be set aside once you experience the results of attentive practice. To learn these techniques, use one of them for a week to allow yourself time to become familiar with the practice. When you are proficient in all of the techniques, you can use them as you feel inclined. Whenever a meditation technique you have been using is not as appealing to you as it once was, or its use does not result in improvement in meditation practice, use one of the other techniques. During long meditation sessions, after sitting in the deep silence for a while, if you begin to come out of meditation but would rather continue with your practice, introduce a meditation technique of your choice to again internalize attention.

1. *Breathing Through the Chakras* – This can be done with or without the use of a mantra. If you want to use your mantra as you do this, it can be useful. First, get into the flow of listening to your mantra. Then, let your awareness be in the spinal pathway and higher brain while the mantra continues. Become aware of your natural breathing rhythm. When you breathe in—letting it happen in the normal way—let the mantra flow with inhalation. If you use a one word mantra, listen to that word or sound when you breathe in and when you breathe out. If you use a two word mantra, listen to the first word when you breathe in and listen to the second word when you breathe out. Listen to a simple word-phrase in the same way. For instance, using the phrase, "I am in God," mentally listen to "I am" with inhalation and "with God" when you exhale. This is a good starting practice because it enables you to work with body rhythms and is not as subtle as listening to the mantra alone. As you become increasingly relaxed and calm, ignore the breathing pattern, forget the body, give full attention to the mantra

and eventually go beyond it.

When you are proficient in this practice, add to it the technique of "breathing" through the chakras. For this, be more aware of the spinal pathway and higher brain centers. Get into the flow of synchronized mantra and breath flows. Then, feel (use your imagination if you have to in the beginning) that an ascending current of prana or vital force is flowing smoothly up through the chakras into the spiritual eye and higher brain as you breathe in. Feel the current descend from the brain to the bottom of the spine as you breathe out. This is called *sushumna* (path of God) *breathing*. Its practice encourages prana to flow through the central channel in the spinal pathway, has a calming effect on the mind, and internalizes attention to allow meditation to unfold naturally. It also awakens dormant life forces in the body which enliven the chakras and nervous system.

2. *Inner Sound and Light Contemplation* – This is a result-producing technique to use after you have become internalized by practice of preliminary procedures, including prayer and mantra. Listen in the inner ear to discern any subtle sounds that may arise. In early stages, you may hear the echoes of environmental sounds resonating. As you listen, you may hear subtle sound frequencies which change from time to time. These may be the sounds of the body's electric forces or the sound frequencies emanating from the chakras. Do not be concerned about the possible origin of the sounds: just give your attention to them. As you intently listen, continue gazing into the spiritual eye. Assume that the ultimate source of the sounds

is the field of pure consciousness out of which all sounds emerge. When you discern a steady, flowing sound, be absorbed in it. Feel ego boundaries dissolve into space. Feel yourself to be one with the cosmic sound   current which pervades the universe. Desire to get to the source of that sound. Contemplate God and the field of absolute Existence-Being. Give yourself to the process until you are settled in a conscious, tranquil state or a superconscious state that unfolds. As you proceed, you may observe light at the spiritual eye. While merged in Om, the sound current, also merge in the light that you perceive. If you hear sound but do not see light, or see light but do not actually hear the sound, work with whatever you do perceive. If you experience sudden shifts of consciousness, surrender to them. Do not be anxious or afraid. Just be open to useful unfoldments that can occur.

3. *Ascending Through the Chakras* – After attending to preparatory meditation procedures, when you are ready to give full attention to your inner work, while gazing into the spiritual eye become aware of the spinal pathway. Still looking into the spiritual eye, *feel* the base chakra at the bottom of the spine and mentally chant "Om." Feel and "listen" to the sound resonating in the chakra. Bring your awareness and *feeling* up to the second chakra. Mentally chant "Om," aware of the sound as though resonating in the chakra. Feel your awareness becoming internalized. Continue in this way, to the lumbar chakra, heart chakra between your shoulder blades, throat chakra in the spine at the neck, and into the spiritual eye. Feel that ascending prana currents are flowing in a steady stream into

the spiritual eye. Let your awareness include the higher brain and beyond. Continue to chant "Om" as you gaze into the spiritual eye, looking through it into the distance of inner space. Gradually cease mental chanting of Om and be still. Listen to the inner sound and continue until you have gone as deeply as possible for that meditation session. Rest in the silence, surrendered in God.

4. *Transcendental Contemplations* – This technique is enjoyable to practice when you have only a few minutes to experience an adjustment in mental attitude and states of consciousness, as well as during more prolonged meditations. It requires the use of imagination but soon takes your awareness beyond mental processes to clear levels of consciousness.

Be relaxed and introspective. Open your mind and awareness to limitless possibilities for expansion of consciousness and increased understanding. Think of a saintly person—someone who lived in the past or who is now embodied, who seems to you to be a personification of noble qualities and spiritual enlightenment—and visualize that person as standing (or sitting) in front of you. Feel their presence with as much reality as you can. Visualize and *feel* that person flowing to you and merging into you. Absorb their spiritual qualities. Experience their mental states and states of consciousness. As you do this, be aware that the process is impersonal. The person you envision is not really there; you are visualizing the personality in order to make the process more real to your senses, mind, and awareness. When when you have an awareness that the spiritual qualities and states of consciousness formerly envisioned in the idealized personality are your own, rest for a while, vividly apprehending the beneficial change you are experiencing.

A Christian might visualize Jesus when implementing this procedure. A Buddhist or Hindu would prefer a saint from their own tradition. One who is a committed disciple of an enlightenment tradition would include the gurus or teachers of that tradition. This procedure is helpful because of the fact that we tend to acquire the characteristics of those whom we revere or admire and with whom we associate. It is not always possible to live in physical proximity to saints. It is always possible, however, to mentally and spiritually attune ourselves to the states of consciousness which are characteristic of illumined souls. By assuming virtues, attitudes, viewpoints, and states of consciousness which are most ideal, we soon become comfortable with them and are able to express them.

An alternative practice, which can follow the one just described or be used separately, is to imagine what it would be like to look upon the world from God's point of view. What is it like to be God? What is it like to be the single, manifesting reality of Supreme Consciousness? What is it like to be the infinite field of consciousness which has a changeless, transcendental aspect as well as expresses as universal manifestation, including as all souls in all realms, planes and dimensions? When peaceful and calm during a meditative interlude, ponder this matter. Contemplate it. Be involved with it. See what you can see. Experience what you can experience. Realize what you can realize. As you proceed, remove your awareness from the various aspects of God and contemplate pure Existence-Being beyond the dualities, outside the field of qualities and attributes. Experience yourself as thoughtless, feelingless, unmodified existence.

When concluding these practices, retain awareness of yourself as a free soul, a ray of God's consciousness with cosmic understanding. Live from that understanding.

5. *Contemplation for Insight and Realization* – Upon progressing to the stage of tranquil mental stillness, contemplate for the purpose of discovery and actual realization. The practice of contemplation is consummated when concentration becomes undisturbed meditation and meditation results in completion or fulfillment of its purpose. Direct your attention to whatever it is you want to know about or experience. Look at it. Ponder it. Identify with it. Be it. If you have unanswered questions about God, your real nature, universal processes—or whatever you want to know about or realize—contemplate and open yourself to knowledge. If you feel inclined to experience and realize higher states of consciousness, contemplate them until you awaken to and experience them with the knowledge that corresponds to them.

If you desire knowledge, insight may not dawn during meditative contemplation, but may surface in your consciousness later when you are not actively thinking about the matter. Desire is self-fulfilling, so if you sincerely desire to know something, you will be able to know it. Knowledge will unfold as insight or revelation or some circumstance or situation will manifest in your life to provide you with knowledge.

When engaged in contemplative meditation for the purpose of direct experience of higher states of consciousness, gently contemplate what you desire to experience while being relaxed and allowing unfoldments to occur. Preliminary states of Self-realization include perceptions of light, bliss, or modifued states of superconsciousness. When so identified with the experience that you feel you are light, bliss, Om, or whatever was formerly contemplated, know this to be spiritually beneficial while not the ultimate state you aspire to realize. An experience of oneness with an aspect of subtle consciousness, or an enjoyable but fixed state of consciousness, is transformative but should be transcended. This kind of experience is described as superconsciousness with support. It is a superconscious experience but is limited because of being identified with something. A higher state is pure awareness with knowledge, without attachment to anything external to itself. Even this, as enlightening as it is, is not the highest condition. Beyond it is total, conscious realization that persists at all times, when we are engaged in meditation and when we are involved with everyday activities and relationships.

With awakened spiritual consciousness, knowledge of almost limitless soul abilities may also unfold. With knowledge, you will know how and when to use these, and when not to. Because no longer egocentric, you will acknowledge that you have no personal power: that you are a ray of God's consciousness and all power is God's.

6. *Spontaneous Meditation: Going with the Flow* – When you have become proficient in meditation practice,

adhere to your preferred routine as long as it is supportive of your purposes. When you no longer need specific
routines, give yourself to the meditation process and go
with the flow. I am, of course, referring to flowing attention to transcendental levels of perception and realization: not to allowing our attention to be caught up in
mental illusions and fantasies.

Be relaxed, internalized, aware, alert, watchful, and
surrendered. Aspire to the highest realizations without
being inclined to force anything. Sit and wait, allowing
adjustments in states of consciousness to occur and being
open to unfoldments for the duration of your meditation
session. If you sit long enough, alert and surrendered to
the process, spontaneous meditation will occur. When
physical and mental obstacles to the natural flows of creative forces are absent, soul awareness unfolds. Spiritual
growth as a Self-illumination process is then realized.

7. *Centering Meditation for All Occasions* – To immediately flow into meditation or to be centered and aware
of your relationship with the Infinite at any time, just be
still and wait until you experience a shift of consciousness. This is especially helpful when you are involved in
daily activities and feel that you are becoming overly
influenced by environmental circumstances or disorganized thoughts and moods. In a secluded place where you
will not be disturbed, close your eyes and be still. Just be
still and wait. You may sit for several minutes before a
change occurs, but it will if you continue to sit. When you
are again centered in soul awareness, resume your
activities. If in a public place, you need not close your

eyes or do anything to attract attention to yourself. In the
midst of outer activity, be still. With practice, you will
learn to easily return to your center just by doing so.

After Meditation: Before Concluding
Your Regular Practice Session

When concluding your practice session, let your meditative calm blend with your mental processes. Feel that
superconscious influences are pervading your mental field:
ordering its actions and contributing to entirely constructive mental states and thoughts. Feel that your mind is
illumined by your soul light. Be self-reminded that your
mind is a portion of Cosmic Mind, God's Mind. Your mental states, thoughts, desires, and intentions interact with
Cosmic Mind. Your mind is a conduit, an outlet through
which divine intentions expressed through Cosmic Mind
can be manifested. Be involved for as long as necessary,
until you feel inclined to move to the next phase.

Let meditative calm pervade your physical body. Feel
that superconscious forces are influential in strengthen-
ing the body's immune system, enlivening the nervous
system, slowing biological aging processes, ordering the
actions of organs, glands, and systems, and awakening
regenerative energies. When you feel inclined, move on
to the next phase.

Extend your awareness to acknowledge the universe
in which you dwell. Know that at the level of mind-body
identification you are relating to the universe. The
universe is a continuum, one manifesting expression of
cosmic forces. It is self-referring and self-providing. Its

energy is not increased or diminished but only expresses change and transformation. As you are in harmony with the universe, so the universe provides for your personal needs. You need not have any anxiety about this. As you are fulfilling your destiny, the universe supports you. Know and feel yourself to be enlightened, rational, healthy, functional, successful, and prosperous.

Don't just think about these conditions and then hope for the best. Assume the states of consciousness, mental attitudes, and feelings which correspond to them.

Acknowledge all people as spiritual beings. Envision the inhabitants of Planet Earth (include all subtle realms and spheres if you want to) and wish them well. Desire for *everyone* their highest good. Feel love and good will and share it.

If you want to pray for anyone, or share your enlightened consciousness with others in a more specific way, think of the person or persons with whom you want to share. Know that where they are, God is, just as where you are, God is. Therefore, you don't have to think about "sending" good thoughts or energies through space. All you do is remain established in awareness of the presence of God for yourself, then know within yourself, on behalf of others, that the activity of the Holy Spirit, God's expressive life, is the operant power. God's grace contributes to the spiritual awakening of others, and to any necessary psychological transformations and adjustments of circumstances and relationships, always in divine order for the highest good of all concerned. You are actually working within your own consciousness to realize that this is so, and sharing your realization with persons whom you include in your mind and consciousness. Continue this contemplative process until you feel Self-complete and know absolutely that all is well now. Be thankful. Be happy. Release the results to God's will. The will, the inclination of God expressing, is always in the direction of orderly growth and fulfillment.

Conclude your meditation practice session when you feel inclined to do so.

Two Examples of Useful
Meditation Routines

With experience, you will discover the meditation routine that suits your personal needs. The following routines may be used as described or adapted as you decide.

1. *A Regular Practice Routine*– Sit in your preferred meditation posture. Practice a few rounds of alternate nostril breathing to help you get centered and settled.

Invoke an awareness of the presence of God. This can be done by silent acknowledgement or by verbal or silent prayer. If you pray, let it be simple and sincere, from the heart, from your innermost core of Being. If you identify yourself with a religious or enlightenment tradition, take a moment to think of the saints in your tradition.

Remember from the outset of meditation that you are a spiritual being grounded in the Infinite. Knowledge is innate to you. You are an individualized expression of Supreme Consciousness. Consciousness has knowledge of itself. Therefore, you have knowledge of your real nature, God, and universal processes. This knowledge will awaken as you meditate. You do not meditate to become something that you are not. You meditate to remove your awareness from body and mind identification so that knowledge can unfold and Self-realization can blossom. Be very clear in your mind and consciousness that you are not to strive to attain Self-realization—you are only to let yourself awaken to it.

Proceed with your preferred meditation technique or routine. If practicing for only 30 minutes or so, use one meditation technique and allow time to rest in the tranquil silence. If meditating a little longer, you may start with one technique, such as mantra, rest in the silence for a while, then use another technique of your choice before concluding with an interlude of stillness and your preferred procedure for ending the session.

2. *Routine for Extended Practice*– Proceed as with the first routine but sit longer during the phases following practice of a meditation technique. Start with mantra meditation if this is your preference. Rest in the silence. Practice breathing through the chakras or chanting through the chakras, concluding with inner light and sound contemplation. Go as deep as you can by surrendering to God and letting your innate urge to have awareness restored to realization of wholeness keep you absorbed in contemplation. After an interlude of stillness following inner light and sound contemplation, if you begin to come out of meditation, again use any of the meditation techniques to internalize your concentration. Aspire to transcendental realizations. If thoughts or mental pictures invade your consciousness, dispel them

immediately. Continue your inspired, attentive practice
for one, two, three, or more hours.

Devotion to God is the most influential aid to success
in meditation practice and to spiritual growth. Without
devotion, one is inclined to be self-serving, or sincerely
engaged in helpful practices from a self-conscious level of
awareness which is limited because of its conditioned
state. Some benefits will be experienced even at this level
of endeavor, but for superior results and rapid spiritual
growth, devotion which inspires the heart and enlivens
faith is vital. Devotion, plus knowledge of meditation techniques—and their faithful application—will result in Self-
realization and full illumination of consciousness.

Part Four

How to Know,
Realize, and Express
God

The heart (the soul), once it experiences awareness of its Source, if nothing diverts it from this communion, sinks deeper by an insensible process of revelation, till it is wholly in God.

Saint Francis of Sales (17th century)

As a result of higher superconscious meditations, superior influences permeate the mental field. Destructive tendencies are dissolved as constructive tendencies become pronounced. Due to its inherent nature, the flow of divine consciousness becomes peaceful and calm.

Yoga *Sutras 3:9,1*

But seek you first fulfillment in God, and live righteously, and all these (material and circumstantial) things shall be provided for you.

The Gospel According to Saint Matthew 6:33

7

*Satisfying Our Desire
to Know God*

OUR OFTEN OBSESSIVE QUEST for meaningful
existence and personal fulfillment, when honestly examined, can be seen for what it is—a misdirected, though
perhaps sincere, endeavor to satisfy the desire of the heart
to know God. To deny this is to continue an agenda of
purposeless behaviors which perpetuate circumstances
that reflect the emptiness of our lives. But in our darkness there shines the eternal ray of hope. When we admit
to our need for understanding, when we follow the urging
of our innermost nature, we can immediately awaken to
knowledge of ourselves and of God, and live with inspired
conviction.

To know God as God is, not as we may have imagined
God to be, is to have all of our delusions and illusions forever banished. It is because of the existence of delusions
and illusions that the soul's perception and experience of
God is veiled or obscured. Delusions are erroneous or
invalid beliefs. Illusions are misinterpretations of what
is perceived. The primary delusion that spiritually
unawake people have is that they are human creatures

independent of God. This causes them to believe themselves to be mortal beings that are born, endure for a while,
and die. Believing this, they either grasp at life while they
have the opportunity, feel themselves to be victims of
circumstances, put up with unpleasant or oppressive conditions and relationships, turn to neurotic or psychotic
behaviors, or sink into nearly unconscious apathy.

To understand the cause of the primary delusion that
blinds souls to the truth, we have to have some understanding of God and the creation process. Thankfully, this
information is available because many enlightened people
have shared it with us through the Ages. We don't have to
believe what they say: we can examine the facts for ourselves and awaken to our own realization. And this is
precisely what we are supposed to do; for if we do not
become knowers of what is true, we will have to be content with being believers only—and belief by itself does
not satisfy the heart's desire to know the truth.

The Creation Process: Emergence of the Worlds and the Origin of Souls

Something does not come out of nothing. The universe
was not produced by a cosmic whim and it is not an illusion. It is not a figment of our imagination and will not
disappear when we cease to perceive it. While not an
illusion, material realms are *illusory* because what we
ordinarily see is not their entirety. Visual perception involves the reception of electro-magnetic energy by our
eyes. This kind of energy travels in waves, which vary in
length. Some electro-magnetic waves, called gamma rays,

are extremely short, measuring only about 4 ten-trillionths of an inch in length. In contrast, electromagnetic waves used for trans-oceanic broadcasts are over 18 miles long. In between are the wave-lengths used for X-rays, infrared radiation, shortwave and regular broadcast signals.

The wavelengths our eyes receive make up what is called the visible spectrum, which may include only about 1 billionth of the existing electro-magnetic field. Receptors in the eyes are sensitive to the visible spectrum wavelengths. Sensation results when this energy is received by the eye and transmitted to the brain. The eye receptors, called rods and cones, convert energy into nerve impulses and send it to the brain to make them meaningful. This is called visual perception. Learning to clearly see what is before us is of value to us in accessing information and relating realistically to the world, and is also a useful spiritual exercise.

When we do not clearly perceive and correctly interpret what we see (and hear) we are at a disadvantage because we are not then in direct communication with our environment. Most failures to perceive clearly are due to inattention or avoidance; that is, we either do not care to observe or we do not want to do so. Even when new information is available to us, because of our personal observation or when communicated to us by another person, we may not actually receive the communication because of inattention or refusal to believe what is presented. This often occurs when new information confronts our habit-bound mental attitude. We may reject useful information or debate its validity rather than open our minds to the possibility that it is true and, perhaps, of value to us.

According to seers of various enlightenment traditions, the universe is an interaction of cosmic forces with origins in a field of Primal Nature which, in turn, has origins in the single, manifesting field of Supreme Consciousness we call God. Out of this field, sometimes referred to as the Godhead, a flow of creative force is projected that, by a process of self-referral, expresses as the field of Primal Nature, the substance of which the universe is produced. In its primary state it is comprised of the original creative force (the Word, Aum or Om), space, time, and particles of cosmic force. From this primal substance all universal manifestations are produced.

The Sanskrit word for this substance is *maya* (from the verb-root *ma*—to measure, to limit, to give form). The word is used to refer to the primal substance and its actions, and is sometimes used to refer to illusory circumstances. In the first instance: "This world is nothing but maya in manifestation." In the second instance: "The devotee's powers of perception are obscured by maya (illusions, the results of misinterpretation of what is perceived) and by delusion (untrue beliefs about what is perceived or thought about)." A person under the spell of illusion may be otherwise reasonably intelligent. A person under the spell of delusion is ignorant on those matters about which knowledge is lacking.

When the light of the Spirit of God shines on the field of Primal Nature, its reflections become individualized or specialized as souls. Souls, being rays of God's consciousness, never become independent, or separate from God. When souls become identified with the field of Primal

Nature their intuitive powers are diminished, causing them to be deluded—and delusion or partial unconsciousness results in attachments to externals. This is how souls become involved with the creation process and proceed to play their varied roles in the drama of life. It is important to understand that we are rays of God's consciousness and, if unaware of this, need only to contemplate the matter and awaken to realization of it. Any seeming sense of becoming united with God as a result of intentional spiritual endeavor or grace is the result our former, erroneous sense of separation, which never actually existed.

From the realm of Primal Nature, creative energy flows outward to manifest the worlds: producing a Cosmic Mental field, sometimes referred to as Cosmic or Universal Mind, and fine, subtle, and gross realms. (See the chart *Cosmic Manifestation and the Involvement of Souls* at the end of this chapter for a more descriptive explanation of this process.) Multiplied trillions of souls become involved with the world manifestation process at various levels. There is no need to feel ashamed about being embodied, or to feel that original involvement with matter was due to intentional willfulness. We became involved because of participating in the process of cosmic manifestation. However, we do have a choice in the matter of whether we blindly identify with mind and matter or whether we awaken to superconscious levels and Self-realization.

Because God is the only expressive reality of Supreme Consciousness, there is no intelligently directed power in conflict with God's actions. There is no personified evil force attempting to thwart evolutionary processes or tempt souls away from their spiritual growth path of destined soul awakening. A committed devotee of God should have no delusions about satanic influences, because there are none. Any personal problems or challenges one might have are due to lack of right understanding which can result in illusory perceptions and misguided actions. When illusions are banished and right actions are implemented, only effortless harmony with the universe results.

Knowing God's True Nature

The Reality, the Being or Presence of God, *is*. The Spirit of God *acts*, or *expresses*. God is the One Life, Being, Power, and Substance in manifestation. God is infinite, without beginning or end. Trying to conceptualize this reality challenges the intellect because the intellect, being a mental faculty, cannot fully grasp that which transcends it. Even so, intellectual examination of the reality of God is useful because it provides a degree of understanding and takes one to the edge of the limits of the intellect where intuition is the next unfoldment. God can be known by intuition, which is not a feeling but an insight—although one might have a feeling-response when insight unfolds. *God is an omnipresent field of consciousness.* This is realized by the soul established in Self-knowledge.

Being a field of consciousness, God is not a person. During early stages of spiritual inquiry it is common for aspirants with a devotional temperament to personalize God as a father, mother, or a higher power which cares for each person. If this is one's approach to understanding and experiencing God, and one's devotion is sincere, a response is drawn from the field of God that may be interpreted as an answer to prayer. In this way, a devotee can have a personalized relationship with God until sufficiently God-realized to clearly know God's true nature and actions. Prayer response, or having needs met without asking for assistance, does not prove that God cares for us as we understand caring expressed by one person to another. The situation and the process does not need to be analyzed and explained: if the relationship satisfies the seeking heart, with results following, that is sufficient. Complete understanding will unfold with illumination of consciousness. When the reality of God is known, all else that needs to be known will be revealed.

Because God's nature is what it is, so long as we have even a faint intellectual grasp or partial intuitive insight of the reality of God, there should be no questions in our minds about whether or not God loves us, cares for us, approves of us, or wants us to awaken spiritually. It is not uncommon for new seekers on the spiritual path—because of their limited understanding, emotional dependency, or prior incomplete or invalid religious training—to see themselves as being in a parent-child relationship with God. This is all right if one is willing to learn and to grow in knowledge and grace. If maintained for years, however, it restricts spiritual growth. A contrasting condition, which is also self-defeating, is an attitude of individual superiority which may be expressed as arrogance and denial of any need for a relationship with a higher power.

Realizing God

If we are not God-realized it is because we have not
given our full attention to God. Many people will say, "But
I do give my attention to God! I do everything I can to
make myself receptive to spiritual growth." Without being judgmental, observe their behaviors when they are
engaged in routine activities. You will see that their
conversations and actions are predominantly related to
secular matters and their behaviors reveal restlessness,
confusion, dependencies, and conditioned responses to
circumstances. Talk with them about God, if you can, and
notice that their intellectual grasp of the nature of God
and how spiritual awakening processes occur, is minimal.
They may want to have a God-relationship, as does
everyone at a deeper level, but they are not preparing
themselves for spiritual growth. They are more attached
to their personality-identity and to habitual behaviors and
existing circumstances than they are to the ideal of spiritual growth. Or, if they are sincere, they may be hopelessly aspiring to a connection with an idealized mental
picture of God instead of knowing and realizing God as
God is.

It is normal for us to conceptualize God when we are
new on the awakening path. As we progress, however, we
need to be willing to renounce invalid concepts and rigid
beliefs about God. When we think about God, our thinking should be rational. We should know—because saints
tell us and in our hearts we are aware of the truth—that
God is the omnipresent field of consciousness out of which
the worlds were produced and by which they are sustained,

and that God is our true, larger reality. God is not Cosmic or Universal Mind: Cosmic Mind is an outer manifestation of God's consciousness which makes possible the universe and its processes. Just as God is not Mind, so we are not the mind we use. To actualize Self-realization we have to remove awareness from mental processes. We do this by surrendering self-consciousness in meditation, or when transcendental awakenings occur at other times.

When every belief and opinion we have about God is renounced, when we are no longer subject to mental conditionings or emotional states, direct realization of God can occur instantaneously. When it does, it is known for what it is. Authentic God-realization instantly dispels all delusions and illusions. If anyone claims to be God-realized, look at their behaviors and circumstances and listen to their words. God-realization is transformative: self-serving behaviors, and words and actions impelled by ignorance of higher realities are eradicated. If anyone claims unique spiritual status, know them to be either deluded or intentionally untruthful.

Help yourself to be open to authentic spiritual growth by ridding yourself of every attitude and behavior which restricts the soul's inclination to unfold. Accept useful information and supportive circumstances while being discerning and using your common sense in practical ways. If what you think and do contributes to your wellness, ability to creatively function, and to your progressive spiritual growth, continue on your present course. Whatever is suppressive or restrictive, renounce: literally "lay it down" and let it go. Cast your mental, emotional, and circumstantial burdens away. Love God and be devoted to spiritual practices and right living while cultivating emotional maturity and rational behaviors. There is no value whatsoever in dramatizing the sentimental emotionalism that some devotees of God mistakenly think to be a demonstration of their sincerity and dedication. Give up your fantasies. At intervals, through the centuries, a wave of interest in mediumship—the presumed ability to telepathically communicate with souls who dwell in subtle realms—sweeps through society. A medium is, supposedly, a mediator between inner and outer realms who passes on information received from beings who have a message to share with people in this world. In recent years this activity has been referred to as channeling. In spite of the fact that all truly enlightened people say this practice should be avoided, many emotionally dependent, undiscerning people become involved with it. Any information provided by a medium comes from their own mind and consciousness, and not from spirits or souls in subtle realms. There is no possibility of acquiring valid knowledge or of experiencing authentic spiritual growth by such involvement. Spiritual masters do not ever speak through mediums.

What about the usefulness of having a guru, a knowledgeable spiritual teacher or mentor, to help us on the path? There is value in such a relationship if the teacher is qualified and the truth seeker is prepared to learn. How can the ideal relationship be established? By individual preparation—by study, right living, and spiritual practice—along with prayer for guidance and constant desire to know and realize God. When the devotee is ready, the right circumstances will prevail. If one is to have the personal guidance of an enlightened teacher, the relationship will unfold. If it is not destined, one's innate intelligence and God's grace will be the guru: the remover of darkness from the mind and consciousness of the devotee. The true guru is God. When God's reality is revealed as a result of a personal guru disciple relationship, it is still God's influential grace that accomplishes the results; thus the fallacy of our searching outwardly for that which can only be experienced by the natural process of Self-illumination. I am referring to the true Self, our spiritual reality, and not the selfhood of conditioned personality.

Many truth seekers err in thinking that they can help themselves to higher understanding by "working out their salvation" without the aid of another, when they really need competent guidance. They seldom read valid truth literature, avoid contact with enlightened people, refuse to heed the spiritual teachings they do have access to, and mistakenly assume that their understanding is superior to that of all others. There is value in learning from others who are successfully demonstrating their knowledge of how to live and how to awaken spiritually. We should not deny ourselves opportunities to learn while, at the same time, remembering the real source of knowledge.

A rightly resolved spiritual aspirant is a disciple on the God-realization path. To be a disciple is to be willing to learn, and to apply what is learned. Knowledge is impotent if it is not utilized. Total dedication to the ideal of God-realization is the way of surrendered discipleship. For total dedication and faithful adherence to the spiritual path, three actions are essential. One action com-

prises the first step to discipleship, the other two ensure
steadfastness on the path:

1. *The Need for Repentance* – To repent is to acknowledge the error of our ways and turn our attention in the
right direction: to look away from all that is incompatible
with our soul-inspired choice to fulfill life's purposes and
awaken spiritually.

2. *The Importance of Commitment* – To commit is to
decide, to agree upon a course of action without doubts or
hesitation. To be committed is to be intentional, decisive,
and one hundred percent dedicated. Commitment trans-
forms repentance into resolute involvement with life-
enhancing behaviors and circumstances.

3. *The Constructive Results of Practice* – After repentance and commitment, we prove our dedication to the
spiritual path by living the truth we know. Practice con-
firms and supports our commitment and enables us to
actualize or demonstrate our understanding at every stage
of intellectual, emotional, and spiritual growth. Included
with our essential practices should be daily prayer and
contemplative meditation.

Our awakenings through the stages of spiritual growth
can be known to us by the changes in states of consciousness we experience, the knowledge that progressively
unfolds, our increasing awareness of our immortality, and
the continuing realizations of God that occur. Adjustments
to superconscious and cosmic conscious states may be

sudden or they may be gradual. After a few years of dedicated endeavor on the path we may be pleasantly surprised to discover that progress has been so steady that, in comparison to attitudes and states of consciousness which were formerly experienced, obvious changes for the better have unfolded. A satisfying perception is that we no longer feel God to be separate from ourselves, or at a distance; instead, we are conscious of living in God at all times.

Unfolding realizations of higher realities result in successive initiations, "new beginnings," as we are provided opportunities to see life from an elevated perspective and are inspired to adapt our behaviors accordingly. We discover that this side of absolute realization of Supreme Consciousness, the possibilities of learning and experience are seemingly endless. This is because the universe is vast and ever-changing, and we bring to it our new states of consciousness and new ways of perceiving things. Only when we are established in pure consciousness do our perceptions of relative phenomena cease. We experience changeless pure consciousness when we meditate deeply. Once grounded in permanent God-consciousness, when not meditating we can inwardly rest in knowledge and awareness of pure consciousness while engaged in thinking, action, and relationship. This is the ultimate spiritual fulfillment—which is not attained, but unfolded from within our consciousness.

Established in this realization we are liberated from past and present conditions which can no longer restrict us. Living, though purposeful, is effortless. Knowledge allows right actions, needs are spontaneously met by the universe at the mundane level and by grace at subjective levels. Religious literature describes this condition as one of salvation: of having been "saved" from ignorance, suffering, and pain as the result of complete spiritual awakening. There is no more seeking, no more striving, no more overcoming. This is not a glorified self-conscious condition —it is the complete opposite of egocentric awareness. At this level, ego-sense is but a fragile faculty which enables the soul to maintain mind-body-world relationships while being viewed by the soul for what it is: a mere convenience for expressing in space-time which does not mar or diminish realization of oneness.

Expressing God

We do not have to demonstrate our spiritual awareness to others to prove anything to them. It is sufficient that we are able to freely express our understanding and skills in ways which are compatible with our personal destiny. We, then, being free, are removed from the influences of the collective human consciousness of the planet. Our continued presence here, when enlightened, contributes to the cleansing of collective human consciousness. There may be practical things we do to be of service to society and the natural order—and if we have the knowledge and resources, we should do so—but the most beneficial offering we can make is the purity of our consciousness.

While in this world, we have duties to fulfill which we assumed by coming here. We can fulfill them while continuing our spiritual growth, and after we have awakened to full God-realization for as long as our destiny requires that we be here. While we are yet on the awakening path, there are three aspects of life to cultivate. After full enlightenment, we nurture them because it is natural for us to do so. A useful guideline for us, while we are still growing, is to observe how conscious, healthy-minded, successful people live, and emulate their actions. The three aspects of our lives that require our attention are the physical, moral, and spiritual. If we are self-disciplined in these matters our lives will be on a firm foundation and we will be well prepared for psychological and spiritual growth to unfold.

To experience personal fulfillment and fulfill life's purposes we need to demonstrate self-responsible behaviors in relationship to four areas of our lives. To neglect even one of them will almost certainly restrict spiritual growth and may result in unhappy experiences and circumstances. They are easy to remember and pleasant to fulfill:

1. *Living with the Full Support of God and Nature* – When we live in harmony with natural laws and are psychologically balanced and spiritually awake, we have the full support of Nature and God's grace enlivens us. Besides living a simple, natural life, it is important to live with real purpose so that we fit into the cosmic pattern and participate in cooperation with evolutionary processes. There is a "right place" for us in the universe. When we are in it, life is enjoyable, personally fulfilling, and nurturing. Any work we do or service we perform is of value to others if it has constructive outcomes, and of

value to us if performed skillfully and with a giving attitude. An indication that we are in our right place in the
universe is the soul satisfaction we experience, along with
an improved appreciation for life and an increasing awareness of growing spiritually.

2. *Satisfying Real Needs* – The universe is self-complete and self-referring: its forces are forever interacting.
At the level of mind and body identification we are involved with universal processes: we interact with Cosmic
Mind through our mind and we interact with the universe
at the physical level. Desires, unless modified or renounced, tend to attract creative forces and circumstances
that result in their fulfillment. Our natural, necessary,
and legitimate desires should be easily fulfilled so that
we can be satisfied and fulfill our purposes with mini-
mum effort. In the physical realm we have needs to be
met: shelter, food, clothing, emotional needs, needs for
relationship, and whatever else is necessary for comfortable, successful living. Natural, legitimate desires for the
satisfaction of needs and even for enjoyment are not
detrimental to spiritual awareness. Insatiable desires and
cravings for experience and things which are inappropriate or harmful are the major problems. They cause
psychological unrest, waste energy, can cause suffering
to oneself or others, and inhibit spiritual growth.

3. *The Benefits of Affluence* – To be affluent is to be "in
the flow" of life and its resources so that whenever anything is needed, to satisfy desire or accomplish a purpose,
it is readily available. Poverty in all of its forms is restric-

tive, a cause of frustration, and prevents us from efficiently accomplishing our purposes. All people, especially devotees of God, should rejoice in being affluent. Renounce all attitudes, beliefs, and behaviors which support poverty. Cultivate attitudes, states of consciousness, and behaviors which enable you to prosper in all ways. God, the only manifesting reality, is expressing as the universe. Therefore, do not claim lack and limitation. Do not believe that it has spiritual value. Make wise use of resources without waste and without grasping or hoarding, but do not be afraid to relate to the universe which is but a manifestation of cosmic forces with their origins in God.

4. *The Importance of Spiritual Freedom* – While attending to the first three matters, include actions which encourage spiritual growth leading to full God-realization and liberation of consciousness. This should be first in order of importance, supported by right living, fulfillment of natural and legitimate desires, and demonstrations of affluence. To be a reasonably happy, healthy, successful, affluent, self-conscious, habit-bound human being, is not to be exceptional or to accomplish anything of lasting value. But to satisfy physical and psychological needs, while expressing ethical and moral qualities and facilitating spiritual growth, is to live righteously and demonstrate higher understanding. Living like this enables us to experience the results of right actions and to know directly how God expresses at fine, subtle, and gross levels of Nature.

The active Power of God that nurtures the universe

includes us in its actions. Our role in the processes of expression and growth is to learn to cooperate with it by
living in harmony with the laws of nature and remaining
receptive and responsive. Until we are spiritually enlightened, right living requires our alert attention and willingness to continually learn. Our spiritual growth is too
important to leave to chance; too intimately related to our
present and future well-being—and the well-being of everyone else—to be uncertain about or neglect. Our states
of soul awareness determine our mental states and both
determine our everyday behaviors and experiences. We
can easily know when our spiritual growth is real or
authentic by how we are living our lives and by what we
are demonstrating in thought, word, and deed.

Superficial study of philosophical principles and regular but inattentive practice of prayer and meditation
routines may indicate an interest in spiritual growth, but
what are the results of such involvement? Are we experiencing steady, progressive spiritual growth and are we
demonstrating it? These are fundamental questions we
need to ask if we are to realize and actualize authentic
spiritual unfoldment.

Here are some guidelines to higher understanding and
to demonstrating our spiritual qualities and capacities.
Respond to the questions and choose to adapt your life to
ideal modes of behavior.

- Are we knowledgeable about ourselves as spiritual
    beings?
- Are we knowledgeable about the reality of God?
- Are we healthy-minded? Are we calm, rational, discern-

ing, cheerful, optimistic, and illusion free?

• Are we emotionally mature? Are we self-responsible and free from addictions, compulsions, and obsessions?

• Are we purposeful? Do we know why we do what we do, and do we perform all actions skillfully?

• Do we have self-respect based on Self-knowledge, instead of self-esteem based on personality traits?

• Do we really care about our personal well-being and spiritual growth? And what are we doing about it?

• Do we really care about other people and do our honest best to encourage them to their highest good?

• Do we really care about Planet Earth? Do we nurture it and do all we can to preserve its resources?

• Do we love God selflessly and endeavor to serve causes higher than our own self-concerned interests?

It is the destiny of every matter-identified soul to awaken from the dream of mortality and have awareness restored to omnipresence and omniscience. A dedicated devotee of God can awaken to this realization within a few years, before the present incarnation is concluded. I pray that you choose to do this. Your committed choice is the most important action: all others will naturally follow, enhancing your life and ensuring fulfillment in God.

Cosmic Manifestation and Involvement of Souls

The processes of cosmic manifestation extend through seven stages of progression. From the field of pure Consciousness-Existence-Being through and as the realms of fine and gross matters, the one Power and Substance is self-referring and self-interacting. The universe is a continuum: one reality expressing according to the relationships and actions of the attributes of nature.

REALM OF PURE CONSCIOUSNESS – The unbounded realm of unmodified Consciousness-Existence-Being, the Absolute Reality sometimes referred to as Supreme Consciousness. Contemplation of this field of consciousness is the highest form of meditation. Being outside the range of relative creation it is incomprehensible to the mind but is directly realized.

REALM OF GOD – The only unfoldment from the field of Supreme Consciousness, with attributes which can be apprehended and experienced as a Being or Presence, but which is not a person. It is Spirit, Intelligence, and Power. Its attracting quality is often referred to as love. When its attributes (gunas) are balanced, objective creation is absent. When they are influential, they regulate cosmic forces which manifest as the universe and its operations.

REALM OF PRIMAL NATURE – When the Word (Om) of God, the creative power-energy-force, flows outward, it expresses as sound frequency, fine cosmic influences, space, and time. Souls are reflected rays of the Spirit of God which shines on this realm of Primal Nature.

REALM OF COSMIC MIND – The initial stage of cosmic individualization and the field in which objective realms exist. Souls involved here partake of aspects of Cosmic Mind and assume a false sense of independent existence or ego-sense.

CAUSAL REALM – Produced from the realm of Cosmic Mind and the pattern for objective realm manifestation. Here, cosmic forces influenced by nature's attributes (gunas) express as five essences of organs of perception (seeing, hearing, touch, feeling, smelling); five essences of organs of action (speech, mobility, manual dexterity, elimination, and reproduction); and five essences of gross manifestation to be perceived (space with fine matters, gaseous substances, fire or transformative actions, watery substances, and earth or gross matters). Realm of magnetic fields.

ASTRAL REALM – Further objectification of fine forces and essences of perception, action, and substances, produce the field of electricities and life forces in which souls can be expressive. This is the realm to which many souls retire between physical incarnations and is sometimes mistakenly referred to as the "true heaven" or final abode of the soul. There are many varieties of states of consciousness represented here. At this level the soul functions through an astral (life force) body.

REALM OF GROSS MATTER – The universe perceived through the physical senses. At subatomic levels it can be viewed as a play of cosmic forces which have their origin in the field of Supreme Consciousness. All aspects of cosmic manifestation are simultaneously present and interacting. Therefore, wherever we are, God is, in fullness of Being, Life, and Power.

The influential attributes of God pervade the field of nature. The Sanskrit word for these is *guna*: influences which regulate cosmic forces. The interactions of luminosity and inertia result in transformative actions, contributing to evolutionary processes which forever occur in the field of space-time.

Awakening Through the Stages of Spiritual Growth

The seven levels of soul awareness represent stages through which we awaken to full enlightenment. Until settled in God-consciousness, various characteristics representative of the levels may be present. To facilitate spiritual growth, renounce psychological characteristics which are restrictive and cultivate states of consciousness and behaviors which are consistent with your highest ideals.

FULL ENLIGHTENMENT – Complete knowledge-realization of God and of universal processes. Liberation of consciousness. When meditating, realization is transcendental. When relating to mundane realms, full enlightenment remains undiminished and all actions are appropriately spontaneous.

GOD CONSCIOUSNESS – Partial or complete knowledge-realization of God with transcendental realizations to follow. Even if mental restrictions persist, their influences are weakened and will be removed. Insightful actions prevent the accumulation of further conditionings. At this level, even with further realizations to unfold, one is liberated from delusions and attachments.

COSMIC CONSCIOUS – Partial or complete knowledge-awareness of universal processes and realization that the universe is a play of cosmic forces. When meditating, perceptions and realizations are transcendental. Comprehension of Primary Nature: the Word (Om), cosmic particles, space, and time. Normal activities and relationships are enjoyed with higher understanding.

SUPERCONSCIOUS – Partial or complete Self-realization. Knowledge-experience that one is a ray of God's consciousness. When meditating, higher superconscious states unfold, allowing perceptions and realizations of God and transcendental realities. Ego-sense diminishes with increasing Self-realization. Normal activities and relationships are experienced without compulsion.

FUNCTIONAL SELF-CONSCIOUSNESS – Healthy-minded, superior human conscious condition. When meditating, the major purpose may be to elicit the relaxation response and experience psychological and physiological benefits only. Normal activities and relationships are rational, nurturing choices. Actions are performed skillfully. Some intellectual understanding of God may be present.

DYSFUNCTIONAL SELF-CONSCIOUSNESS – Mental confusion and conflicted emotional states are common. Egocentricity prevails. Meditation may be practiced in the hope that a degree of inner peace may result. Illusions are common: also attachments, dependency, addictions, and self-defeating behaviors. Actions are irrational and behaviors are unpredictable. Neurotic needs, complaints, blaming, and irresponsibility are common—as are fantasies about everyday matters and higher realities. Subconscious influences dominate mental and emotional states.

UNCONSCIOUS – Mental dullness, apathy, and boredom are common. The physical body is assumed to be the real being. Awareness of spiritual matters is absent. If religious, prayer is usually directed to a conceptualized form or aspect of God. Normal activities and relationships are routine, as necessary or as one is inclined by desire or whim. Intellectual powers are limited. Memories, habits, and learned or acquired behaviors dominate lifestyle. Small-mindedness and self-righteousness may be dramatized.

Every soul eventually awakens from unconsciousness to Self-knowledge and realization of oneness in God. Personal aspiration to spiritual growth is a helpful influence to this end. The soul's innate inclination to awaken is a determining factor. Right living and spiritual practices speed up the process.

The Vital Centers and Their Characteristics

The seven major vital centers through which soul consciousness is processed are along the spinal pathway and in higher brain centers. They are of the astral or life-force body or sheath, and serve as focal points through which soul forces flow to perform various functions. Prana (life-force) frequency characteristics at each center can be subjectively discerned. States of consciousness and their influential behaviors can also be related to the centers (Sanskrit, *chakras*).

SEVENTH VITAL CENTER – In the upper brain but not confined to it. Light perceived when meditating is "as of a thousand suns." Soul awareness is pure consciousness, Absolute-Existence-Being. The Sanskrit name *sahasrara* means "thousand-rayed" because of its radiance. Soul awareness is wholeness. Behaviors are compassionate. Transcendental perceptions and realizations are spontaneous. Soul liberation results.

SIXTH VITAL CENTER – Between the eyebrows, reflecting light from the medulla center at the base of the brain. Light perceived as a dark blue orb with golden halo and centered with brilliant white light. White is the light of Spirit; blue is the light-frequency of Cosmic Intelligence; gold is the light-frequency of Om, the Word, the Sound Current. Its name *ajna* means "command." It is the controlling center for prana flows. Soul awareness here is God-realization. Behaviors reflect this.

FIFTH VITAL CENTER – In the spine opposite the throat. Perceived as "misty" with sparkling lights. The psychological state is inspiration to knowledge. Powers of intelligence and intuition enable the devotee to comprehend subjective realities and categories of cosmic manifestation: to be "in the world but not deluded by it." Its name *vishudda* means "pure." A possible challenge at this level is blind misuse of knowledge. The devotee should aspire to go to higher levels.

FOURTH VITAL CENTER – In the spine opposite the heart. Perceived as blue light. Its name *anahata* means "unstruck sound" because the Om frequency here is like the sound of a pealing gong after it has been struck. The "door" between subjective and objective levels of awareness. If spiritually quickened, the devotee functioning through this chakra desires to be Self-realized and enters into a program of discipleship training for the purpose of experiencing a God-relationship.

THIRD VITAL CENTER – Opposite the navel. Inner light perceived, reflected in the spiritual eye, is reddish. Its name *manipura* means "city of gems." The psychological state is egoism and soul abilities may be expressed as creative use of mental faculties as well as executive skills. If self-centered, one will want to exercise power. If somewhat spiritually awakened, abilities will be used for noble causes: to fulfill purposes, satisfy needs, and constructively benefit society.

SECOND CHAKRA – At the sacrum section of the spine. Inner light perceived may be white, with geometrical patterns. Its name *swadhisthan* means "abode of the Self" because kundalini (dormant soul force) is confined here when not awakened. Psychological states may reveal evidence of sensuality, confusion, fantasy, fascination with sights, sounds, and feelings, and curiosity. One may want to "reach out" and touch the environment, to experience and "taste" it.

FIRST CHAKRA – At the base of the spine. Inner light perceived may be yellowish. Its name *muladhara* means "foundation." Psychological states may reveal restlessness, insecurity, drive toward self-preservation is almost entirely outward. Attention is almost entirely outward. Awareness of or interest in spiritual matters may be absent. Persons strongly identified with this, and the second and third vital centers, need to be spiritually quickened or awakened to levels of soul awareness at which higher possibilities can be apprehended. Spiritual aspiration, prayer, meditation, virtuous living, and the companionship of spiritually aware associates are helpful for this.

8

Living in the Infinite

THE FULLNESS OF THE REALITY OF GOD is infinite and inclusive. The all-pervading field of God is consciously, simultaneously present everywhere. All worlds, creatures, and beings exist in God.

Whenever you feel alone or in need of anything, think or speak these words: *Here and now, God is. God is around me as a vibrant, living presence and as me at my innermost level of being. God is the reality and substance of everything I see, touch, and relate to moment-to-moment.*

At first, these words (or ones of your own of a similar kind) may be thought of as an affirmation, used to order your thoughts and provide a degree of reassurance. As you intuitively grasp the essence of what you are saying, your soul nature will be quickened as you awaken to the truth and reality of God as God is.

We are inclined to supplicate God or to endeavor to make ourselves pleasing and receptive to the Presence so long as we feel ourselves to be independent beings apart from the whole. This is a natural, human conscious approach, and starting at this level of need for higher understanding is a good beginning. It reflects our humility, our recognition of the fact that our egocentric view of self in relationship to life is inadequate to enable us to be entirely self-sufficient or truly happy. It is evidence of our honesty; that we are admitting to ourselves that we, as mind-body creatures, are insignificant in comparison to the cosmos and to God's omnipresence, omniscience, and omnipotence. Our acknowledgement of the superficiality and meaningless of our self-conscious lives is thus a beginning of the end of our denial of spiritual Selfhood and God. Turning away from delusive thinking because of choosing to identify with the source of all good is the one, decisive act that, in a single stroke, weakens the influences of our illusions and allows us perceptions of possibilities perhaps formerly only imagined.

To say that God is present at some places but not others, is to affirm an untruth. Likewise, to say that God "cares" for some people or circumstances more than others, is to reveal our lack of understanding about the real nature of God. God, being wholeness, is not capable of concern or disinterest: attitudes which only have relevance to a mind confused by beliefs of duality. Every soul has the same opportunity to awaken and to know as God knows. Thankfully, past behaviors have nothing to do with our being able to awaken to the reality of God. As we awaken, all that formerly clouded the mind and consciousness and contributed to flawed perception and inappropriate behavior, is immediately removed so that expressive soul qualities are enabled to unfold.

As we become familiar with progressive spiritual growth episodes that occur, we become increasingly aware that our self-disciplined behaviors are for the purpose of removing self-centered attitudes and actions from the playing field of our lives so that grace can have its way. While inspired to do what we can to live with knowledgeable purpose in harmony with natural laws and supported by spiritual practices, as we go deeper into God we notice that useful inner changes and supportive outer unfoldments of circumstances and events occur—not because of what we do, but because of what we are able to allow. This is not to suggest that we can avoid our necessary personal disciplines and duties to ourselves and others: only that, what we do with intention because of our self-responsible attitude, enables us to live with the rhythms of life. Living like this makes us increasingly receptive and responsive to the actions of grace.

Expressive grace is not a reward for our good intentions or constructive behaviors. Grace is the natural unfoldment of life to support its own purposes and actions, in which we participate when we are in tune with the Infinite. Cosmic processes are ever in motion because of interactions of cosmic forces which, as do all natural forces, have their origins in God. Heaviness or inertia, transformative movement, and actions which contribute to luminosity and purity, are the three fundamental characteristics of the underlying, triple qualities of the natural order which reveal the influences of cosmic forces. These qualities are also present in our minds and bodies, as they are in every relationship and circumstance we experience. To learn to live in harmony with them, it is recommended that a spiritual aspirant choose states of consciousness, mental attitudes, thoughts, emotions, relationships, environmental circumstances, life-purpose, and actions which contribute to increasing the influences of the qualities which nurture total wellness and spiritual growth.

Whatever is nourishing to mind and body, whatever supports healthy-mindedness and wellness and vitality, and whatever contributes to wholesome, harmonious relationships in all aspects of our lives, should be chosen and included in our lifestyle. Everything that is debilitating or creates stress and conflict, should be avoided. The ideal is to be in harmony with circumstances that are supportive of us and, by so doing, be assisted by the currents of evolution to fulfillment.

It is actually easier to grow spiritually and be successful in everyday endeavors and relationships than not to do so. It requires extensive effort to cope with frustration and failure and the other hardships common to people in a spiritually unawake, self-conscious condition. An unpleasant truth is that many people who aspire to spiritual growth are approaching the project with the same self-defeating attitudes and behaviors which are already contributing to the problems that burden their lives. Once sufficient right knowledge is acquired, if it is used effectively, personal accomplishment and spiritual growth rapidly follow. This is something illumined people have long known: that higher knowledge and its right application quickens one's spiritual evolution.

What can save us from habitual, self-defeating actions is inner renewal reinforced by resolved determination to live an entirely constructive life. This means choosing a natural food diet, attending to self-care routines, setting aside time each day for study that renews the mind and adds to our knowledge, regular meditation practice, and living with enthusiastic, high resolve. These things we should do as duty. We will not then be subject to moods or whims, but will learn to live skillfully in cooperative relationship with the universe.

How and Why the Universe is Able to Meet Our Every Need

The universe, as God's manifesting energy-consciousness, is self-complete and self-referring. Its energy and substance does not increase or decrease: it undergoes transformational changes. Being complete within itself, it can only refer to itself. Therefore, there is no lack in the universe and there are no transformations which are in accord with its laws that it cannot express.

As spiritual beings, using a mind that is a portion of Cosmic Mind and functioning through a body comprised of cosmic forces and natural elements, we can be in harmony with universal processes. To live in harmony with universal processes is referred to in religious literature as abiding by the ways of righteousness. Doing this, with spiritual awareness and clear understanding, enables us to experience the spontaneous, effortless support of the universe. Hence the advice given by Jesus (*Matthew* 6:33) to persons seeking to know how their daily needs could be met, to seek first a knowing relationship with God and to live righteously: the results of which are that the universe responds accordingly.

How does this process work? It works on two levels. First, when we are in harmony with life's processes, we live more effectively and are able to accomplish our purposes efficiently. Second, *when we are established in soul peace, anything that disturbs it draws a response from Cosmic Mind and the universe to meet the need so that we can be restored to peace.*

It matters not what the circumstances are that disturb our spiritual tranquility. It may be our awareness of need for food, shelter, transportation, relationship, the cooperation of others, a problem that is pressing or a circumstance that needs to be harmonized, a desire to accomplish or to have something, more knowledge or spiritual growth—whatever it is that causes our soul peace to be disturbed—the universe will move to meet our needs and restore us to realization of wholeness.

Let your life be like this. Remember the benevolent Power that nourishes the universe, including you, and learn to cooperate with it. To the extent that you are open to life, life is responsive to you. Do these things:

- Have the courage to live.
- Accept the fact that living can be natural, spontaneous, and enjoyable.
- Serve the cause of evolution.
- Be on friendly terms with a friendly universe and care for, and nurture, Planet Earth.
- Make wise choices.
- Be appreciative of the blessings of life.
- Actualize your compassion by serving others.
- Solve all problems with spiritual understanding.
- Do the things you should do and renounce behaviors that are not worthy of you.
- Be your real Self and follow your soul happiness.

- Don't pretend to be a victim. You are a spiritual being, innately endowed with limitless capacities.
- Cultivate the virtues.
- Educate yourself and be as knowledgeable and functional as you can be.
- Pray and meditate every day.
- Choose a lifestyle which is supportive of your worthy purposes and spiritual aspirations.
- Abide by the ways of righteousness.
- Wake up, grow up, do your duties, and flow in harmony with the rhythms of the universe.
- Be happy. Be thankful.
- Be awake in God. Live consciously in the Infinite.

Concepts that pass through our minds may have temporary, inspirational value, then soon be forgotten. Peruse the pages of this book from time to time, to refresh your memory and be motivated to inspired actions. God is your life. You can realize your divine Self and live freely in the Infinite by responding to your innate urge to do so.

Glossary

An understanding of the meanings of the following words will be helpful to a more complete comprehension of the text of this book.

Absolute: The nondual field of Supreme Consciousness. The transcendental field, devoid of modifications yet containing the potentiality of expression. It remains ever-the-same behind the veil of matter and mind.

actualize: To "make real" or bring into expression or manifestation. We actualize our potential when we demonstrate it. Our aims in life are actualized when they are fulfilled.

astral realm: The subtle sphere of electric matters and life forces pervading the cosmos. Souls come into physical embodiment through the astral realm and may return to it between incarnations.

causal realm: The finer sphere of electric forces and magnetism pervading the cosmos, which preceded astral and physical realms in the process of world manifestation. Souls may reside here between astral incarnations and awaken from this sphere to celestial and transcendental levels of perception.

chakra: Wheel. In yogic teachings, an astral focus for the distribution of prana (life force) from the brain through these vital centers along the spinal pathway. The seven principle chakras are located in proximity to the brain, medulla oblongata, cervical region of the spine in the neck, dorsal region of the spine behind the lungs and heart, lumbar region behind the solar plexus, sacrum (lower back), and the bottom of the spine. Being astral in character, they emanate sound-frequencies consistent with their functions which may be heard by the meditator who listens in the inner ear. The prana frequencies may also be perceived at the spiritual eye center as varied, colored lights. The spiritual eye reflects the lights from the medulla center at the base of the brain as ascending currents of prana converge there during introspective contemplation. The chakras are sometimes illustrated by artists as lotus flowers, with opened petals representing the blossoming of unfolding soul consciousness. When dormant soul forces become active in the body as a result of awakened spiritual consciousness, they flow upward through the chakras to the brain, contributing to enlivening of the body's forces, improved powers of concentration, and expanded states of consciousness.

Christ: Derived from Latin *Christus*, from Greek *Kristos* (*Khristos,* anointed, and *khriein,* to anoint). In secular usage the word was used in reference to the religious rite of anointing with oil. Christian mystics may use the word in reference to the aspect of the Godhead which is actively expressing in the universe to endow it with divine qualities and regulate its operations. To be Christ-conscious is to be sufficiently, spiritually awake to experience or realize awareness as one with this aspect of God in cosmic expression.

consciousness: In metaphysical literature the word is used in two ways. 1) Consciousness as awareness of an object. We may say, "I am conscious of my thoughts, feelings, and environment." 2) Consciousness without an object: as self-existent. Our "states" of consciousness are determined by their degrees of

clarity. Unconditioned soul consciousness is pure. Self-realization is experience of ourselves as pure consciousness.

cosmic consciousness: Realized awareness of the oneness of
all life: that everything in manifestation is an expression of
Supreme Consciousness. As with other perceptions or realizations, cosmic consciousness may be partial or it may be more
pronounced. It may unfold gradually or suddenly, providing
knowledge which is self-revealed rather than acquired by a
formal learning process. Cosmic consciousness can be cultivated
by renouncing egocentric attitudes and by aspiration for spiritual growth. Natural living and spiritual practices can facilitate the emergence of cosmic consciousness. To whatever
degree experienced, cosmic consciousness is illuminating and
transformative.

disciple: *Disciple* and *discipline* are from Latin *disciplus*, and
discere: to learn. A disciple is a person who is willing to learn
and apply learning to fulfill purposes. A disciple on the spiritual path learns to facilitate awakened spiritual consciousness.
Some obstacles to discipleship are: incapacity or inability to
learn; egocentricity; mental perversity which causes one to
distort information and use it for self-interested purposes;
laziness; provincialism or small-mindedness; addictive behaviors; and purposelessness.

God: The only expansion from the field of Supreme Consciousness; endowed with qualities and characteristics—the Godhead,
out of which the Word (Om) is projected to manifest the worlds.
God is the omnipresent field of consciousness which includes
everything within itself but which is not influenced by world
processes.

God-realization: Actual knowledge-experience of God that may unfold progressively or suddenly. The soul, the true Self of every person, is an individualized unit of God's consciousness. God-realization is the result of awakening, not of attainment in the sense of acquiring.

guru: Sanskrit, *gu,* darkness, and *ru,* light. The reality of God is the light that removes delusion from our minds and awareness, either directly or through the agency of an enlightened teacher. In secular usage the word means teacher.

heaven: Originally a cosmological term that identified a region of the universe but which came to function as a vehicle of religious idealism. In ancient Near Eastern thought, "heaven" identified a region beyond the observable cosmos, which pointed beyond itself to transcendental realms. In ancient Greek mythology, Zeus dwells on Mount Olympus. The Old Testament refers to heaven as God's abode from which sovereign rule is exercised and to which the faithful righteous are finally welcomed. The New Testament reflects a modified version: Heaven is God's creation in which he resides as well as a condition of blessedness experienced by the spiritually prepared. Various religious sects have their own concepts of heaven and its opposite place or condition, hell. Illusion-free understanding allows one to know that one's degree of Self-realization and God consciousness determines circumstantial conditions.

initiation: Literally "a new beginning." Whenever we learn something new, more of the allness of life is apprehended. Spiritual initiation may be a spontaneous awakening to higher states of consciousness or may be an occasion of formal instruction and spiritual awakening. In the latter instance, the initiate is taught guidelines for living, informed about spiritual growth processes, is usually instructed in prayer and meditation practices, and is encouraged to commit to a life of dedicated service to God and continued spiritual endeavor. Meditation instruction may include the imparting of a prayer formula, a mantra, or other specific techniques to be used. The new initiate is then considered to be a disciple of God on the enlightenment path.

mantra: A word, word-phrase, or sound which is "listened to" during preliminary stages of meditation practice, to serve as a focus for concentration and to prevent attention from being involved with sources of possible distraction, including random thought processes. When the meditator's attention is attracted to the mantra, perfect concentration follows without effort. Eventually, the mantra is discarded or transcended and meditation proceeds spontaneously.

maya: The primal substance of which the natural worlds are formed. It is comprised of the creative force of Om, space, time, and cosmic particles. One characteristic of maya is its form-producing tendency. The other characteristic is that it is truth-veiling: when a soul identifies with it, awareness becomes clouded and intellect becomes veiled. Maya is the cause of illusory perception in deluded souls but is not itself an illusion.

meditation: The process of flowing attention to one's object of contemplation or to transcendental realities so that insight can unfold and Self-realization can blossom.

metaphysics: From Greek *meta,* beyond, after, and *Physika* (Aristotle's treatise called *Physics*), hence Aristotle's writings "after physics." The word is now used to refer to philosophical theories and principles that deal with matters which transcend (or are outside of) the range of objective nature.

Om: The primary, creative force from which all cosmic forces are produced. Also called the Word, as in *The Gospel According to Saint John* 1:1: "In the beginning was the Word, and the Word was with God, and the Word was God." Yogic literature refers to it as the sound current, which is to be listened to as a mantra when meditating, then transcended.

prana: First unit of cosmic life force which pervades the natural order and enlivens it. The prana-frequencies active in our bodies are aspects of our soul force.

pranayama: A procedure, usually in relationship to regulating breathing patterns, to enable one to harmonize the flows of prana in the body. A simple form of pranayama is alternate nostril breathing. There are others for different purposes.

prayer: Reverent petitioning or an endeavor to commune with God, the results of which are experienced as demonstrated circumstances and more spiritually satisfying states of consciousness. Prayer can be simple mental or verbal interaction with God, as God is imagined to be or as God is known to be. In a higher sense, it is a volitional act of turning away from self-sense to allow a more comprehensive realization of soul qualities and higher realities to be actualized. Devotees of many faiths have experienced the transformative effects of surrendered prayer. Many have realized God directly by prayer, without knowledge or practice of other procedures. For this, the devotee prays through all moods and thoughts, then rests in contemplative stillness to know and experience God as God is.

Self-realization: Actual knowledge and experience of one's real, spiritual nature. Self-realization is awakened to, rather than created or caused. Self-realization makes possible true knowledge and realization of God.

soul: A ray of reflected light of the Spirit of God that shines on the field of Primal Matter or maya. In some philosophical systems, a more precise definition is that the reflected rays of spiritual light are individualized units of God's consciousness which, when they become identified with Cosmic Mind, are referred to as souls. In this context, souls are in need of having awareness restored to flawless purity. This is accomplished by awakening and Self-discovery.

spiritual eye: A term used in reference to the place between the eyebrows to which attention can be directed when meditating. Doing this effectively internalizes attention. Prana flows which ascend the spinal pathway during meditation converge at the base of the brain and are reflected in the spiritual eye, sometimes called the third eye.

superconsciousness: Awareness experienced when attention is free from involvement with conditioned mental states and states of consciousness and which is, therefore, superior to them. Superconsciousness is soul awareness. Preliminary stages may be modified by mental conditionings or clouded awareness. During meditation, when mental impulses and actions are quieted, and the meditator remains alert, superconsciousness naturally becomes pronounced.

yoga: As a practice: to bring together all aspects of body, mind, and personality so that functional, skillful living can be actualized and Self-realization facilitated. The end of yoga practice is flawless God-realization or enlightenment.